RELIGIOUS
MISUNDERSTANDINGS

AHMED HULUSI

www.ahmedhulusi.com

RELIGIOUS
MISUNDERSTANDINGS

AHMED HULUSI

www.ahmedhulusi.com

KITSAN PUBLICATIONS
Istanbul / 2002

RELIGIOUS
MISUNDERSTANDINGS

AHMED HULUSI

Translated by
AHMED BAKI

www.ahmedbaki.com

First published by KITSAN in Turkey in 1999
Reprinted in 2000 and 2001   2002

ISBN 975-7557-79-X

Cover design by Ahmed Baki
Author photograph by C.K.

Translation of "DİNİ YANLIŞ ALGILAMAK"

KITSAN Publishing House,
Ticarethane Sokak No:41
34400 Cagaloglu - Istanbul / TURKEY
Phone: ++90 212 5136769
Fax: ++90 212 5115144
http://www.kitsan.com

Printed in Istanbul by Bas-er Press Ltd.
Phone: ++90 212 6133055

For the latest revised edition of English, German and French
translations of our publications as well as their originals in Turkish
and for any correspondence, you may contact the authors direct
via e-mail or visit Ahmed Baki's Web site on the Internet at
www.ahmedbaki.com

E-mail to **Ahmed Hulusi**   : **ahulusi@ahmedhulusi.com**

E-mail to **Ahmed Baki**   : **message@ahmedbaki.com**

TABLE OF CONTENTS

PREFACE

I begin with the name "**ALLAH**".

May *Salaat* and eternal Peace be upon HU's **Rasul Mohammed Mustafa** who informed us the *Deen* at the sight of "ALLAH".

Dear Friend,

The *Deen* of **ISLAM** (Religion) is entirely based on the recognition that **ALLAH is AHAD as announced in the Koran**.

With respect to the authority of the Koran, ISLAM is not one of many religions of the world but is **the *Deen* at the sight of ALLAH** (*ind'Allah*).

To understand and evaluate this essential fact, we need first to read and understand what the name "**ALLAH**" refers to as a basis in the **Koran** and in the **teachings of RasulAllah** *aleyhessalaam* who communicated It to us.

The whole universe is an intelligent system and the *Deen* is the information that explains this intelligent universal system. None of the approaches that are not principally **based on the understanding of oneness of ALLAH** can be connected with the **Deen at the sight of ALLAH**.

The greatest enmity on the *Deen* as well as on the peace of humankind has been to speak **ABOUT the contents of the *Deen* without knowing the basic concept denoted by the name 'ALLAH' as informed by Mohammed** *aleyhessalaam*.

They who try to guide people IN THE NAME OF (!) a religion with creating impressions of religious authority have in fact been throwing speeches only about <u>a God and a religion in their own imagination</u>. Without the recognition of the meaning that the name "ALLAH" refers to, they not only make people lose interest in and stay away from **Allah**, but also from **Hu's Rasul** and **Islam**, knowingly or unknowingly.

Recognizing and having effective faith in what is denoted by the concept ALLAH and the System HU created, require first a spiritual consciousness that totally accepts, embraces the entire creation and contemplates the life with the eye of ALLAH. The goal for such a faithful and evolved consciousness is to see past the creation to observe what is called as **the Creator** within the essence of everything.

However, due to the mass of misunderstandings and misguidance built on the **misconception about what is denoted by the name ALLAH**, the very basic proposals of the *Deen* such as acceptance, forgiveness, connection, unity and oneness have been misinterpreted and even been replaced with completely contrary actions in the name of the religion, such as complaining, blaming, expelling and separation.

It needs to be understood before all that there is no god out-there in the sky that expects favor from his followers on earth and that will reward some deeds achieved to gain merit. The original understanding of the *Deen* as informed by **Mohammed** *aleyhessalaam*, <u>who confirmed all the Rasuls and the revelations prior to him</u>, can never be considered as another religion that came after or against some other religions.

One must know that all religious classifications and separations, titles and labels pertain to this physical world only and none is going to have effect in the spiritual dimension beyond the five senses. However, the state of our consciousness as to live to accept, confirm and experience the undivided wholeness of all that IS and its authority on everything that happens in life, is what will construct an entire future for us in the spiritual dimension.

An open mind and a spiritual consciousness are gifts bestowed on human, who can be refined from misunderstandings and conditionings that veil the experience of the reality of life.

Spiritually conscious person is not content with the limitations of the five senses. He seeks to see beyond the physical appearances and to understand, experience the undivided wholeness of Essence within everything. He is one who acts first toward his inner self and he experiences the enormous power of thought and belief. Therefore spiritual practices take an important place in his life. He avoids actions that make him feel separated but he approaches life with a loving and enlightening attitude. Life is endless for him and he views death as a transition into a new dimension. He is constantly thankful for all that was given and he shares and serves generously.

For those who are ignorant of the truth, however, there is a God out-there or off in the sky somewhere, which they either accept or deny! They limit themselves to the five senses in thoughts and beliefs, and as a consequence feel themselves and everything separate from all others. God is likewise separate and He (!) will someday hold people accountable. They only know how to act toward the external world and the goal for them is to live to prove themselves and control the world, as life is in this physical universe only in their eyes. They are not thankful inside, as they don't see themselves receiving any gift, assistance or forgiveness. The ignorant is firm that his existence will end with this lifetime. Always ignoring the invisible reality in all aspects in favor of the visible world is the general attitude of the ignorant.

It must be known that at he root of all afflictions that human suffers, lies his unawareness of the unseparated Wholeness of all that IS. There is no other way of liberation for human other than RECOGNIZING and ACCEPTING the meaning that is informed through the name ALLAH, RECONSIDERING the *Deen-i* **ISLAM** and RECONSTRUCTING his view about life under such an understanding. Therefore nothing in this world serves humankind more vital than the **information** about truth shared generously and unconditionally without any expectation of return.

There is no forgiveness waiting for someone who ignored the information and the preparation for a life of the spiritual dimension of consciousness, as there is no god afar off who may forgive.

Freedom from the physical restrictions of the five senses into an eternal peace through accessing the dimension of cosmic consciousness is only possible through correcting our misunderstandings about the information communicated to us by RasulAllah **Mohammed** *aleyhessalaam* within the framework of the *Deen-i* **ISLAM**.

This book, I believe, will be a helpful tool to achieve this goal, which is a collection I prepared from some of Author Ahmed Hulusi's recent writings and previous works under seven basic titles for the particular purpose of presenting the new readers with several basic themes in a single publication.

If we are able to evaluate all this information, let us be thankful for that and let us try our best to express our gratitude by sharing it generously with a loving, serving and enlightening attitude. May "ALLAH" enable us all to appreciate "Islam' correctly as the *Deen* at HU's sight and have effective faith in what RasulAllah informed us...

* * *

AHMED BAKI
6.6.1999
Istanbul - TURKEY
E-mail: baki@ahmedbaki.com
http://www.ahmedbaki.com
http://come.to/allah

FOREWORD

SYSTEMATIC THOUGHT

My Dear Friends...

With reference to what **Allah** made this poor humble (*faqir*) aware of...

Our holy book **Koran** *al Karim*, the **Rasul of Allah** and the *Deen* of **Islam** have been unfortunately misinterpreted by quite a large majority in our current day.

Moreover, as we consider every subject separate from one another, and as we do not analyze the available data in a systematic way in association with others, we cannot become aware of that misunderstanding.

And this is the point that distinguishes a **thinker** from the rest.

For a thinker, there is no separate subject that can be considered by itself. They are certain that every subject should be thoroughly considered and evaluated within and in connection with the other subjects that surrounds it.

Same as in a puzzle, each segment should find its own place, and at the end should achieve to present the whole image.

The important fact for a non-thinker, - whatever his title is- is, however, to collect in a box, hundreds or thousands of segments that achieve the image. He is satisfied with only a small piece of image in his hand, and he can even blaspheme others who may refer to a single image that shows up as a whole after the integration of segments.

Yet, the dull-witted on the other hand, who judges and finds fault with the inharmonious alignment of segments' side by side, blames the picture itself, saying, "it does not mean anything, it is a nonsense", considering those who fail to understand the puzzle at their hands.

The Deen speaks to two types of believers…

1. The dull-witted that hold onto it with fear and without understanding, in order to rescue himself…

2. The people of reflective mind who aim for evaluating the *Deen* with understanding.

Reflective minds evaluate both the **Koran** and the **Rasul of Allah** not only in terms of very current day of its descent but in a **universal dimension beyond terms of time** and try to understand it in a form that speaks even to a thousand years later.

They dwell on the deep understanding of the Statements with regards to how they should be understood for all lifetimes, rather than their literal meaning and their application within the frame of their time of descent.

They try to comprehend the 'soul' (spirit) of a sign that descends and a statement that is communicated. They seek the reason as to why, how and for what purpose that a sign, a word or an expression is communicated to make a change...

It is this seeking that makes the reflective minds reach to the "SOUL" of the Koran and the VERITY (*haqiqat*) of Rasulness. This concludes at the attainment of the fact that:

"The *Deen* at the sight of ALLAH is ISLAM."

May Allah bestow on us all, the aptness to attain the ***Deen*** **at Hu's sight** (*indAllah*), that is **Islam** and to rid ourselves of our vicious, restricted evaluations.

AHMED HULUSI

6.4.1999

Raleigh, NC – USA

E-mail:ahulusi@ahmedhulusi.com

http://www.ahmedhulusi.com
http://www.allah-sufism-islam.com

WHICH IS CORRECT?

Although the results to be suffered would be the same, an Arab's denial of the **Rasul of Allah** and the **Koran** will not be the same as the denial by a non-Arab.

Being an Arab, someone can reject some information that came to him in his own language, because of his incapacity to understand it.

A non-Arab however, can in fact confirm or reject the understanding of its *translator* only, in a way, for he cannot get the point within reach without the translation of someone else.

Besides...

Taking into account the recent criticism of some paper columnists, you can also have some idea about people's level of understanding. Some columnists state that this is a society of 70 percent dull-witted we are in, while others pull this number upper.

How reliable do you think that the **information recounted by people** can be within a dull-witted community, in which repeating the words of someone or other is considered enough to be a "**person of wisdom** (*ilm*)" while people lack the ability to **reflect** (*tafaqqur*) = **deep thinking** as they grow up with a mentality that education is to give something word for word?

What do you think about the level of "**knowledge**" (*ilm*) of those people who are poor of *ability to think systematically*, who speak in a mode based on **so-and-so person's fatwa** (decision after his interpretation) whenever that decision favors them, and who try to hide their ignorance saying "**only Allah knows it**" whenever they cannot find an answer?

How can it be possible to address to tomorrow by means of the repetition of yesterday?

"*The religion of Muslimism*" in our day appears to be the acceptance of "**using force on people to put the orders of God into practice**" through the repetition of old clichés within the management of an authority.

A public speaker of that acceptance utters the following view:

"**I have a militarist understanding in religion!**"

It means such a religion of Islam that it is based on a chain of command and control, you see!

How do you then account for (where do you leave then) the rule (*hukm*) that "<u>**communicate only, you are not one to force them**</u>"?

"**Faith**" (*iman*) **is from the ordainment of the Creator**!

"**Proposals**" are made for the aim that it may be a vehicle to help one manifest what the Creator has already bestowed upon.

Everybody will live the rest of his or her lives eternally through receiving every time the result of their former (recent) states and behaviors!

In the System, rules the firm and fix (unchangeable) order of the Creator!

No matter what the excuse may be, no one will be able to receive the return of what he or she has not achieved at all.

Therefore, we need to put away the "*militarist*" understanding with regards to the theme of **RELIGION** and comprehend the wisdom (*hiqma*) in the understanding of **Rasul of Allah** that "**one should communicate and not force**".

<u>**We need to perceive the "Islamiyyat" through a window enabling us to view directly the Rasul of Allah and what he brought, instead of looking through a window of a *tariqat* (sect) or *jamaat* (congregation, community).**</u>

Someone comes up and "*denies god*"! He does it rightfully...

Because, he is denying the "*god*" that a dull-witted has informed him!

Modern Sciences have made him comprehend that **there is no "*god*"**. As regards the one that is referred to as "**Allah**", not even the one who speaks is aware of what it is that the one who listened to could be expected to confirm it. Actually, none of the rational persons who are capable of thinking, can deny the one that is referred to as **ALLAH**!

Someone comes up and rejects the "**prophet**"! He may do!

Except those who accept a "*prophet*" by way of conditioning, learning by rote, by suspicion (*wahm*), every intelligent brain will normally deny a "prophet" described as a "postman - ambassador"!

What difference has such a description from an Alien ambassador from outer space?

While you fail to explain that being a **Rasul of Allah** has nothing to do with that "*postman-ambassador*" type of "*prophethood*" and while even you have not understood it properly, what can you expect from the other person?

During the *khutba* (addressing) in the *salaat Cum'a* I attended last week, someone given the title "*imam*", was mentioning that:

"*Allah and the angels in the sky...*"

If the Religious Affairs become a Government office, then of course, *Allah and* _the angels will possess some chairs in the sky_ in due course of understandings!

Seeing such a state of affairs, somewhat reasonable people will hence keep away from such nonsense and begin to gather around some other "_imams_" with more knowledge and thought.

Here is the basic fault:

Provided that the case has nothing to do with an "**enmity toward religion**"...

Instead of censuring religious education, the facts and the truth of the "**Deen**" must be given to people and they must be given help to keep them away from mistakes [and misinformation].

By condemning something by saying it is "_bad-dirty_", no solution can be brought; inversely, problems are hence turned to a Gordian knot (deadlock).

If you are _not_ bringing to light what is "true" and "accurate" at the same time when you are suggesting that something is inaccurate, your sincerity will of course be doubted and your <u>dishonesty</u> may be questioned; and in due course the "truth" among your talks will be wasted and gone.

If you want to prevent some mistakes, explain why it is a mistake if your power of knowledge (_ilm_) allows you, instead of directly bringing forbiddance!

Otherwise, you will be attached a label of "<u>**fascist with democratic appearance**</u>"!.

In the eyes of people of reflection with at least a fair level of intelligence, "**COMPELLING**" is nothing other than the **admittance of a lack in knowlege** (*ilm*), a primitiveness and an underdevelopment.

Of course, it will be difficult for you if:

You are not able to explain that the reason of the unfoldment of quality of **Rasul*ness* of Allah** is the manifestation of **Allah**'s knowledge (*ilm*) in "**human**", whom **Allah** is "**closer than the vein of his neck**" [as the Koran informs] as "**Allah**" makes every atom of the creation existent from within Hu's own **knowledge** and **power** (*qudrat*)...

If you have not understood that what is known as the "**Angelic universe**" is a dimension through which every atom is brought into the actuality as that dimension takes its origin from the characteristics of the knowledge (*ilm*) and power (*qudrat*) qualities which are the verity (*haqiqat*) of all existence...

If you have not realized that the **Koran** is a "**survival guide**" brought to decode the **BOOK** of **READING** known as "*ummul kitab*", that teaches man himself in connection with the System and Order created by the one that is referred to as **ALLAH** and that provides man with solutions for his problems...

In that case, you will find a lot of dilemmas within the "*Religion of Muslimism*" that you took refuge in, but you will either quit reflection with a "**FEAR of beat**" in future and take everything granted as told; or perhaps you will have to refuse it entirely because of this.

However, if that denial will not push you toward investigating the truth, you will not be able avoid from paying its cost, when your excuse that "*you had not been informed about it*" will be invalid!

Are you so <u>blind</u> as to see that there is no place for any excuse in the nature of the Creator?

* * *

Chapter 1

The **RELIGION**

Entrance into knowledge is
with knowing ALLAH,
as knowledge without knowing
ALLAH is a vain effort.

A.H.

WHEN WILL YOU WAKE UP?

"<u>**The Speech of the System**</u>" are these writings…

Of course, those who cannot "**read**" the <u>**system**</u> will find it difficult to grasp some of these writings with their brains that are restricted and conditioned with the perspectives based on prevailing relative judgements of the past.

Also, I have mentioned in some of my writings that I am writing these for the most part for the next generations. For the people of our day, even half of what I have written seems more than enough.

I have no suggestion other than "keeping silence" for those brains that, due to their failure to perceive and read the System, talk about the imperial commands in a hard cover book, which were sent to a postman by the gods created in their images.

What do you think we are forewarned by **RASULALLAH** with that, "<u>**In the end of the world, not even a single believer (mumin)**</u>

will be found among a thousand people filling a mosque"?

I am not expecting anything at all from those who keep carrying out deeds by way of imitation without conscious consideration and waste their lives with the chit-chats of Sufism on "*who said what?*" and "*what said the other*"!

So many years are past since leaving the hope of accession into the field of Sufism that was portrayed through saying,

"If you will not allow the loss of your head and life,

Keep away, do not step in this field of strive!"

Consider how some people necking out their heads into it, have soon escaped in a hurry without even looking behind themselves and then sought for a relief in the expectation of assistance from their gods and their postman.

"So many gardens I have seen ruined entirely!"

At that time I have understood that it is not the day of talking on Sufism with those heroic men in appearance, but is the time of **saving the faith** (*iman*)!

Angels in heaven, Satan on earth, a postman at the door with the book in his hand, and a God that sends them from a corner of galaxy!.. Hell is at one side of galaxy; heaven is at the other far side!!!

The "*Deen* of **Islam**" has been deviated into that understanding and then has been assumed and accepted as the "*Religion of Muslimism*".

Religion is turned into a stock in trade that the *religious men of authority* sell.

The new Religion of Muslimism has been exalted by elevating the religious declarations (*fatwa*), up to an equable level with verses of the Koran or the sayings of RasulAllah!

On the other hand, they who did not accept the religious declarations (*fatwa*) or the patrons of *fatwa*, have been labeled as "**heretic**" (*qafir*) and "**erratic**" (*zindik*)! They have been left out of the "*Religion of Muslimism*", *alhamdulillah*.

The leading persons of Sufism have almost been made gods, their words being taken ahead of the sayings of **RasulAllah**!

A new religious conception has been reproduced upon the understandings that:

"My sheik (religious mentor) is greater than your sheik and will beat yours"...

"My school is superior to yours"...

"My religion is more exalted than yours"...

"My trousers (!) are better smoothed off than yours"...

Pretending to be a *sheik* through the accumulation of information is now enough for receiving the treatment as a **person of total awareness** (*ahl-i irfan*) from common people.

The requirement of the "*Religion of Muslimism*" is yet nothing other than wearing either dress with veil or baggy trousers.

In this new understanding of religion, it does not matter at all if one knows what and why to believe in (iman)... It is more than enough for the people of that new religious understanding to exercise gymnastics five times a day, to suffer hunger for certain hours while still continuing to eat the raw flesh through backbiting, to deliver the old used items from home or office in order to get more of them from god, and in addition to relieve the soul with a tourist journey to Makkah!..

If you have also built a school and educated students with that information in order to have more layman to learn these and apply into their lives, you are already put on pedestal by them.

What about your "certainty" (*yakin*) for what is denoted by the name "Allah?

What is a "RasulAllah" and how one becomes "RasulAllah", what is its outcome? What is its difference from a Postman-messenger prophet?..

What is the reason that belief in "Angels" is so important and is mentioned right following the belief in "Allah" in the sign of the Koran and in the "*amantu*"? Where are the angels? What do we lose if we do not know of them, what do we earn if we know?

What is the "Book"? What was the book of RasulAllah *aleyhessalaam* to be "READ"? Why is it a must (*fard*) for all believers to "READ"?

What is Hereafter (*akhirat*)? Where is it? How is it? Why is it?

What does it mean that both "good" and "evil" are from "Allah"? And why?

What is the revival (*baa'th*) that follows the taste of death (*mawt*)? What does it mean to witness (*shahadat*)? How and what can be witnessed? Why is "witnessing" necessary for a human?

Why does the *Deen* of ISLAM NOT ALLOW IMITATIONS?

These are the foremost and most basic questions to be answered in order to be one that have accepted the "***Deen* of Islam**".

If you are not able to give answer to these questions, you will be wasting your lifetime in this world by consoling, relieving and deceiving yourself with the "Religion of Muslimism" and believing in a *postman-messenger prophet and his god* and as such will pass away.

My **Allah**, **the Witness** (*Ash-Shahid*)! All I can do in my life is to comprehend that I am your "**servant**" and to contemplate that my **servitude for You** continues "**all the time**".

As an effect of my servitude, I have been manifesting what You have willed, foreordained and made easy, with your grace.

I have been implementing my servitude through bringing to words (communicating) the requirements that You wished, with your servants that You have crated as You desired.

"Allah, the Knower (*Alim*)"... "Allah, the Successor (*Wakil*)"... Allah, my Lord (*Rabb*)"!

"Fa aynama tuwallu fasamma wechullah"!

Allah, who created each of what HU created in the most perfect form, with a reason (*hikmat*), appropriately as due according to the purpose of creating in order to exhibit Hu's will.

Your wisdom can never be questioned!.. Servant is yours, the field is yours; existence is yours and reason (*hikmat*) is yours!

Fault, error, loss, defect, mistake are in "**me**"!

Gracefulness (*lutf*), bestowal (*ihsan*), forgiveness, assistance are only in "**YOU**"!

Endow us with the understanding, comprehension, acceptance and living the effect of the "**Deen of Islam**", and make it easy for us sharing it. Save us from being one of those who deny what comes from Your "**RASUL**"...

Save us from being one of those who observe the reliance on the *Deen* and the truth (*haqiqat*) as an investment for Hereafter (*akhirat*) and therefore **oppress their own souls**.

Allah, the Independent of the universes (*Gani*)! Make it possible for us immediately to grasp in what and for what reason the "faith" (*iman*) is necessary for us?

"*Inna kulle shayin biyadillah*"!

"*La hawla wa la quwwata illa billah*"!

* * *

AN UP-TO-DATE UNDERSTANDING OF RELIGION

Dear Friend,

You are going to meet with some new ideas in this chapter. It is our sincere hope that you may reflect upon them as free from prejudice as possible, make investigation and discuss with intellectual minds around yourself to find out the truth. The rest is up to you alone. For our part, there is none other than respect for your decision.

My friend! With respect to the latest contemporary scientific data explored by two of the world's most respected scientists, Neurophysiologist **Karl Pribram** at **Stanford University** in the USA and Physicist **David Bohm**, a protégé of **Einstein's**, THE TRUE NATURE OF THE UNIVERSE IS A "WHOLENESS," THAT IS ENTIRELY COMPOSED OF QUANTA ENERGY AND

DESIGNED HOLOGRAPHICALLY".[*] In the same way, HUMAN BRAIN is a substance composed of waves of frequencies, that operates also holographically... **"DEATH' is nothing other than the survival of consciousness through a transition from one level of hologram into another**."

Human brain sculpts a type of "luminous body of frequencies" (body of light), that is known as **"SPIRIT"** (*ruh*), by means of converting the bioelectric energy gained from the analysis of nutrients into sort of a luminous energy (frequencies). At the same time, the brain not only records all its mental activity onto that "luminous body" in form of frequencies (as

---

[*] A hologram is a three-dimensional image. It is produced with the help of a laser light is split into two separate beams. The first beam is bounced off the object to be photographed. Then the second beam is allowed to collide with the reflected light of the first. When this happens they create an interference pattern which is then recorded on a piece of film. To the naked eye the image in the film looks nothing at all like the object photographed and is composed of irregular ripples known as interference patterns. However, as soon as the film is illuminated with a bright light source, a tree-dimensional image of the original object reappears. Unlike normal photographs, every small fragment of a piece of holographic film contains all the information recorded in the whole. The image is often so convincing that you can actually walk around a holographic projection and view it from different angles. But if you try to touch it, your hand will waft right through it and you will discover there is really nothing there.

meaningful waves), that it sculpts hereby, it also spreads out them all over space.

Since each person's brain constructs his own "spirit," the view known as **"reincarnation"** which argues that a spirit reenters a physical body after its transmigration from one, is absolutely a baseless view. (Reincarnation is a **Hindu** belief in origin.)

The **Koran**, Holy Book of **Islam**, portrays **"death"** as an event to be **"tasted"** and emphasizes in the **Chapter of Mu'minun,** (signs 99-100) that **it is impossible for a human being to come back to earth by rebirth, once the death is tasted**...

Let us return to the point of Holographic Universe for more, back again... Experimental evidence has shown that subatomic particles, that compose our physical universe, move as ghostly images and possess what appears to be holographic property. One of he thought-provoking findings **Bohm** determined is that the **subatomic particles are thoroughly interconnected with each other. Such an interconnection indicates that the universe viewed as composed of "parts" is in fact organized by a basic WHOLENESS.**

It means that subatomic particles are not independent things and are not separate from one another. Behavior of the parts are actually organized by an implicate deeper order as a whole. After all his determinations, **Bohm** arrived at the conclusion that **"the universe is a kind of giant hologram."**

Based on the hologram principle, every particle of the universe fully contains every quality observed in the whole universe. That is, **every portion of the universe enfolds the whole**. Everything in the universe is part of a continuum and each thing fully enfolds the properties of another thing, and it is even the same "another thing." **The reality so beyond "our own concept of world" has a WHOLENESS undivided, unbroken and unfragmented into parts.**

Bohm explained his new findings of QUANTUM PHYSICS in his new field what he called the **QUANTUM POTENTIAL**, a new dimension:

- **At the subquantum level, the level in which the quantum potential operates, location ceases to exist. All points in space became equal to all other points in space. We call this property "nonlocality." All of space, all particles are nonlocally interconnected**.

- **Just as every portion of a hologram contains the image of the whole, every portion of the universe possesses the whole information. This means that the information is equally embedded in the whole "nonlocally" as a whole**.

All these explorations reveal a reality that **there cannot be a "GOD-OUT-THERE" residing in some places of space**!

Besides, according to the **Koran**, the Holy Book of **Islam**, "**THERE IS NO GOD, THERE IS ONLY ALLAH ALONE**," and that **ALLAH is AHAD** (Chapter of Unity, 112:1), meaning the single **ONE** unbroken into fragments, pieces or components. The existence of a separate second being beside HU's existence cannot be thought, and HU's wholeness cannot be assumed as a totality composed of "parts" or "pieces." In consideration of this fact, pantheist view never refers to what is denoted through the name "**ALLAH**".

Everything as abstracted out and viewed as SEPARATE THINGS in the level of our perception originates from within the existence of ALLAH; however, Hu's wholeness is not a totality of many things. **There is ONLY "HU" in reality**. The observation of multiple reality of everything in the universe is an illusion and an imagination resulting from the perceptive capacity of the observer, from the way he looks.

The basic reality being an undivided WHOLENESS has appeared as "**a multitude**," which is an abstraction standing out in our perception by our way of viewing the universe, by making "**attributary separateness**" within the capacity of observers according to Hu's will. In absolute reality, **there is only ALLAH alone**, and nothing outside Hu's self...

At the holographic level of quantum, all things are actually inseparably interwoven, and life and consciousness are enfolded throughout the totality of the universe. Dividing the universe up into living and nonliving things also has no meaning.

There are countless numbers of dimensional levels of existence and intelligent life forms in the entire universe; each being composed of various waves of frequency. We, the humankind, do in fact form only one of those countless dimensional levels of such a multilayered holographic universe.

In every level of existence in the universe, life keeps going eternally in constant transformations from one dimension into the other. However, there is no absence for any individual that has once existed. Once that a human being is an existent intellectual unit, his life will continue for ever, passing through levels of different dimensions.

The last **Rasul** *Hazrat* **Mohammed** *aleyhessalaam* has communicated this universal truth through the science that came to him **from within his own TRUTH** that is **ALLAH,** by means of READING the System, and emphasized the **ONENESS of ALLAH** 14 hundred years before our day, so as human beings should not worship any gods. He emphasized that human beings will continue their lives after a transition from the dimension of biological body to a dimension, a realm of spirit bodies (that is sort of a luminous dimension).

Besides, he explained the necessity of achieving some practices referring to the fact that the preparation for such a level of life can only be made during one's lifetime in this world, and suggested people some proposals about it!

The **Rasul** has already forewarned people and completed his duty IN THE NAME OF ALLAH. Nobody after him has an authority to speak or to judge IN THE NAME OF "Allah." Everybody can speak ABOUT "Allah" and ABOUT the *Deen* at the level his science allows him but never IN THE NAME OF ALLAH!

The Prophet's proposals are for human beings, whose lives will continue beyond death, and not for any States or Governments! In the life after death, there is not any State, but persons as individuals. The *Deen* has come so that "**people**" should prepare themselves for the conditions of life beyond death.

The *Deen* (Religion) has nothing to do with the States, Governments and political regimes. It never addresses to States. Religion holds persons responsible individually, not any State or any Government. And every person as an individual is responsible directly towards the Rasul **Mohammed Mustafa** *aleyhessalaam*, who communicated the *Deen* to us; no one being responsible towards any other person, any establishment, community or society, no matter whatever religious title, career or fame they bear.

With reference to the **Koran**, "**there shall be no compelling**, no compulsion" in the *Deen* of **Islam**.

The proposals have already been provided for persons to benefit them in the life beyond death. He that follows them with a peaceful heart shall do it to his own good, he that gives no heed to them, shall do so at his own peril taking over its consequences in the life beyond death. Pressure and compelling give rise to hypocrisy, therefore they have not been allowed in **Islam**.

The proposals offered in Islam are not a "software package" as that one should either obey them to the full, or not at all. This is completely an out-of-Islam type of understanding and interpretation. Each person practices as much of them as he can to his benefit, and the rest is his personal loss.

None of the deeds practiced in return for a payment is respected' in the *Deen*. (If a practice is turned a profit on, it is not valid in the *Deen*). A practice that will not be achieved in case it is not paid for is obviously done for commercial purposes, and it can never be considered as "*ibadat*" (praying)!

There is no people's class of religious authority in the *Deen-i* **Islam**. No matter what religious identification or term of address one holds, nobody can interact between a person and the **Rasul** who made the communication. **Nobody is required to follow anyone besides the Rasul. The** *Deen* **of Islam is by no means in the monopoly or in the registration of any person, any establishment**. Each person is in need of learning his own religion adequately from the original sources as it is and practice his understanding as much as he can. If a person has been misinformed, he is responsible for this and therefore cannot have an excuse for it.

All the practices known as *ibadat*, which were passed onto us through the Rasul, are **completely based on scientific realities**. They are never aimed at pleasing the heart's desire of a god off in the heights above, afar off (beyond) us. **ALLAH**, who made the universe existent out of nothing, is not in need of any one's practice. Just like the food you take are aimed at supplying your physical body's needs, the practices called as *ibadat* (prayers) are related to the needs of your life beyond death. They are related to the "knowledge" and "energy" that your brain power records onto your, in a way a luminous body of frequencies, that is your spirit.

The practices that are carried out can be divided into two as physical and mental in view of their benefits. Benefits gained physically empower mental activities and subsequently expand the brain capacity, and thus empower the person's spirit.

Constant repetition of words, a practice known as "*zhikr*," makes you realize the **universal qualities,** that are the meanings of ALLAH names, which existed **holographically** in your own being, **through expanding your brain capacity. It increases brain capacity and energy**. For instance, the repetition of the word "**Mureed**" in a certain number of times a day, which is the **Name of Allah's quality of being "will**," increases the **person's will-power**. The repetition of the name "**Quddus**" in addition to the name "**Mureed**," results in a person quitting all sorts of his malicious habits. High tempered, rowdy, heart-breaking, excessive people lacking in self-control and persons of a nervous (tense, irritable) temper dissolve to a tolerant character shortly after they start repeating the Name "**Haliym**." All these come true as brain cells are programmed in corresponding frequencies produced in the brain. This fact was scientifically proved as a laboratory experiment recently and it was published in an article with the signature of **John Horgan** in the **December 1993** issue of **"The Scientific American"**.

The more a person's brain capacity is increased, the better he realizes and knows ALLAH as being the truth of the attributes that unfold through himself.

"**ALLAH**" is not a god afar off, but is the name of the Great One (*Akbar*) who brought everything into existence from within Hu's own being, WITHIN Hu's own knowledge (*ilm*) through Hu's knowledge, while there existed nothing. In the **hologram** system, Hu exists fully in every particle; put in Sufi (*Tasawwuf*) terms, "Hu exists in every point with all Hu's Attributes (*Sifat*), Names (*Asma*) and Hu's Essence (*Zhat*)."

At the extent we could broaden our brain capacity by way of carrying out practices on this path, we will realize and find ALLAH within our own beings, and attain Hu within ourselves...

There are countless types of intelligence within countless levels of wavelengths in the universe. Some types of those live beings that live on a subtler level of reality occupying the same space as our world, has been named as "***jinni***" in the Religion. They deceive humans whom they associate with, commonly by introducing themselves as "**aliens** or **UFOs**" coming from outer space, and/or as the spirits of deceased people and even of saints (*awliyah*). **The most common trick they play is to impose people who follow them, the idea of "reincarnation", that is a Hindu acceptance and is defied by Islam**. Their ultimate desire is to render human beings pass away into the luminous dimension of life beyond death with impotent luminous bodies, that is, powerless spirits; so that they may easily obsess and capture humans in that dimension. To reach this, **jinni** always keep people conditioned to such ideas as to cause people keep away from the teachings of the **Koran**.

Witchcraft and Magic are endeavors completely out of Islam. The **Koran** rejects them.

The Rasul set the first basic principle as follows:

"Make it loved, do not arouse hatred; Make it easy, not difficult!"

The most serious enemies of the *Deen-i Islam* are those who, by creating a religious impression, show the requirements as utmost difficult and make people lose interest and stay away from **Islam**, **Allah** and **Hu's Rasul**. In the life beyond death, they cannot dare to look at the face of the Rasul, even they will not be able to get near him!

Islam is built completely on scientific realities. However, due to the social conditions during the time it came, most matters were to be explained "**in parables and metaphors**" via symbols along with matching similarities. For this very reason they cannot easily be placed onto reasonable bases in our day and thus they are often greeted with denial. Nevertheless, if it is considered and examined free of prejudice and with a scientific view, it will be clearly seen that **Islam** involves not only the facts to illuminate the science of our age, but also of ages to come.

It is unfortunate that some people of superficial interest in this matter, choose to waste their brief lifetimes with chit-chats in prejudiced manners about matters concerned with the physical life of the Prophet which is built on the circumstances, traditions and customs of that age, instead of discussing the facts in scientific or intellectual dimension.

For our part, it is important to appreciate the events carefully in a realistic way!

We should consider what a great reform it was for the **Koran** to set a limit of a maximum of four wives in a community in which, before the **Koran** was revealed, a man could possess unlimited numbers of women and sell, even inherit them for his sons such as his **property**!

How can a normal intelligent person claim the excessive passion of a person for woman, who got married to a forty year old widowed at the age of twenty-five and stayed with her alone for twenty-five years when he was still content with her ever when she was sixty-five and himself fifty?

If one fails to understand and appreciate *Hazrat* **Mohammed's** being "**Rasul**" informing us of "**Allah**" as the essence, the origin, the truth of existence; one should, if nothing else, try to understand his eminence in his being "Rasul" performing a service to mediate for the basis of people's happiness in an eternal life beyond death . . . so as one should put aside the chit-chat of the matter.

We should realize the fact that such an eminent person has not been sent to establish world sovereignty or to establish a Religious Government, to bring an

economical or social order, briefly, to provide a worldly sovereignty, a wealth for people.

Nobody's race, language or color, be him whomever, has any importance at his sight! The foremost thing he is concerned with is the fact that in case **people could not understand the reality of life beyond death because of ignorance**, they will have to suffer greatly as a result of their failure to prepare for that future life adequately...

Yes my friend!

Modern man is one who is open to information (*ilm*) and to the new, who **listens and reads without prejudice**, feels free to discuss over his ideas, and who examines matters at logical integrity.

The *Deen-i* **Islam** within its original context has a peculiarity to address to the modern intellectual man. If so, you should do research and appreciate the *Deen-i* **Islam** through the works of contemporary intellectuals and thinkers who prepared them unconditionally, free from commercial anxieties.

In this booklet, we have tried to communicate some of the information about religious teachings in a highly summarized way based on the explanations of the **Rasul** and the **Koran** in association with parallels in the contemporary scientific data. You can in fact find answer to all possible questions about these facts in all details in the books that we have written.

Since we don't have another chance of coming back to earth over again, we need to make best of our current lifetimes.

We hope that, when we face the realities tomorrow, we shall not regret of our lifetimes past here because of what we have lived in this world and what we have not.

May Allah make us realize and comprehend the truth of life.

And may Allah make it easy for us!

Chapter 2

ALLAH

I have tried to explain to mankind
what the name ALLAH refers to,
but they instead updated their
version of GOD with this
information.
A.H.

SEE THE DIFFERENCE:
"ALLAH" is not a "GOD"

Hazrat **Mohammed**, who informed the *Deen-i* **Islam**, defies the idea of a GOD and emphasizes that **there is no GOD; only "ALLAH" exists**, based on the **Koran** *al Karim*... **Are you aware of this fact**?

In this chapter you will clearly see why the concept "**ALLAH**" informed by the **Koran** *al Karim* is completely different from any concept of a "GOD" in all other beliefs.

There is **a version of GOD** in the minds of everybody, of almost all from the most primitive to the civilized.

It is **such a GOD** that we love at times or feel angry with, at other times. There are even times when we judge and condemn HIM for his wrong deeds and misgivings somehow. To tell the truth, we often fancy Him almost as a sweet, plump grand-dad or as an enraged, wrathful sultan who sits on a star **FAR ABOVE US,** or maybe in some other places of outer space!

There are some with a broader sense however, who argue that there cannot be such a "GOD" in reality as that in people's imagination, and say that "they do not believe in God." Such people are therefore called "godless" or "atheist."

Though in fact, neither atheists who do not recognize a god, nor those who had an image of GOD in their minds in association with what they heard about and were preconditioned, are aware of "**MOHAMMED's ALLAH**" at all!

Therefore, assuming that the concept of a "**God**" is the same as "**ALLAH**", people substitute their concept of "God" for "**ALLAH**" in a manner of as if making something better. In fact, what they do is right as they are indeed speaking about the image of **THEIR "GODS" in their minds** rather than "**ALLAH**" and the true concept of "**ALLAH**".

We must certainly know that...

RasulAllah **Mohammed Mustafa** *aleyhessalaam* and the **Koran** *al Karim* emphasize this important fact;

Neither is there a **GOD OUT-THERE** nor **AFAR OFF YOU; there is ONLY "ALLAH"**...

The sign in the **Koran** that:

"**They did not understand ALLAH with the understanding due to ALLAH**" (22:74) signifies our negligence about this fact...

It should be known that:

The words "**GOD**", "**DEITY**" in English and "**DIEU**" in French and "**GOT**" in German do all mean a concept of "**being to worship**" as their equivalents in other languages...

This means, people denote **a GOD or a DEITY out-there** through all these words!

Yet the word "**ALLAH**" is a **PROPER noun for a BEING**! It is therefore that, to mean that Being or to introduce that Being we either denote Hu through some of Hu's attributes or point out Hu's attributes through some of names. However, all those names signify only a few of the qualities of that Being and define Hu only in terms of such mentioned qualities.

For instance, people call this poor humble as "**HULUSI**". This is a proper noun for him... This name **cannot be translated into any other language**... It has always to be "**HULUSI**" whether in English or in French...

The same way as this, the word "**ALLAH**" cannot be translated into any other language nor can it be replaced with any other word, as it is a **proper noun** for a **Unique Being**...

In point of fact, as seen above, while all other names denote a "**concept of deity**", only the word "**ALLAH**" denotes that Unique Being for it is a proper noun for that Being.

Hence, none of the words implying a concept of deity can be replaced with the word "**ALLAH**"...

Those who substitute the word "GOD" for "**ALLAH**" have been falling into such an error for either their ignorance or their unknowingness, or they have a lack of understanding and perception to truly evaluate this fact...

If a person imagines or assumes the presence of a separate "being" associated with "ALLAH", no matter what term of address or conception it is given when "**ALLAH**" is mentioned, that is a Being known with this proper noun and is free from any concept of a "**fragment**" (*juzz*), he will fall into a state of polytheism (*shirk*), that is associating partners with ALLAH. In such a case, he will have acknowledged a "GOD" because of veiling the truth "**ALLAH**"...

The following is the sign to warn such a person against such a state:

"*SET UP NO GOD BESIDES ALLAH, lest you incur disgrace and ruin...*" (17:22)

Here is another warning about the same situation:

"*INVOKE NO GOD WITH ALLAH.*" (28:88)

It is meant that, as the true Absolute Being that exists is "ALLAH", you should avoid acting heedlessly toward the meaning of concept "**ALLAH**" and from falling into the state of setting up a "GOD" through assuming the Being denoted through the name "ALLAH" as a "god afar off you"...

Through the acceptance of a god out there or afar off you, you will unintentionally get out of the meaning of the concept "**ALLAH**" and will be trapped in a **"god" image**...

As a consequence, you will make yourself deprived of the "**unity**" (*wahdat*) comprehension that the **Koran** *al Karim* informs!

This will be "**the greatest oppression (*zulm*) done onto your own soul**"!..

Hazrat **Mohammed** *aleyhessalam* (peace and blessings be upon him) proclaimed as a result of the Divine Inspiration (*wahey*) that he was the *Rasul* of Allah and he began to do his best to warn people not to worship a god...

The reality that *Hazrat* **Mohammed** emphasized and began with suggesting to men through the message as "**THERE IS NO GOD, THERE IS ONLY ALLAH**" (*La ilaha ill-Allah*) was formulated as the **Word of Oneness** (*Kalimat-it tawhid*).

The meaning of the statement "*La ilaha ill-Allah*" constitutes the basis of **Islam**.

"*La ilaha ill-Allah*" can be interpreted simply as; "**there is no god, there is only ALLAH.**"

If we analyze the meaning of each word:

La ilaha: "*La*" means "**there is no**"; "*ilah*" means "**god**," that is "**a being to be worshipped**." Hence, "*la ilaha*" means "**there is no being to be worshipped.**"

Now, let us pay attention to this fact at this point: The "Word of Oneness" begins with "*La ilaha*" and so, a definite degree is emphasized right in the beginning: "**There is no being to be worshipped**" *(LA ILAHA)*.

Then, **ill-Allah** follows as an explanation: "*illa*" meaning "**only,**" "**ALLAH.**" It does not even say, "there is **ALLAH**"; it simply says "**only ALLAH.**"

This is the fact revealed from this statement first as a primary meaning: "There is no god to worship!"

After definitely stating that **there is no god afar off somewhere that to be worshipped**, "*illa ALLAH*" follows.

The word "*illa*" can be understood as "ONLY" in its usage here.

When using "*illa*" with the word "**ALLAH,**" it must be definitely understood as "ONLY"; because there is no other existence apart from "**ALLAH**" that ALLAH could be compared with it, or could be measured and defined in connection with it. This theme is widely explained in our coming book entitled "***WHAT MOHAMMED READ***".

It is because of this reason that if the word "*illa*" comes in connection with the name "**ALLAH,**" it must always be translated as "ONLY."

From this point of view, the translation of the Word of Oneness into English should not be as "there is no god but **ALLAH**," but "**there is no god, ONLY ALLAH.**"

Only after then that the concept of *wahdat* (UNITY - ONENESS), which is the system [fundamental principal] of thought and belief that the *Deen* of Islam informs, should be grasped accordingly.

This statement informs that there exists only "**ALLAH**" and **ALLAH** is not a god to worship. Because it is definitely stated at the beginning that "*la ilaha*" — **there is no being to be worshipped!**

Therefore, what is informed through the noun **ALLAH is not a GOD** outside human **that to be worshipped**, nor a GOD-afar-off, outside, far away from all existing things that we perceive they are there!

If we precisely understand that "**ALLAH** is **AHAD**," we will then see through insight (*basirat*) that **there is not a duality of "an ALLAH**" and "**a separate universe**" all aside!

That is to say, it is not such that there is **ALLAH** and also there are universes [that exist independently]!

In other words, such a consideration as there are some universes we live in, the cosmos (*alam*), and there is a separate GOD-out-of-all-things and at the farther side, is absolute nonsense!

MOHAMMED's ALLAH is not a GOD!

MOHAMMED's ALLAH is "**AHAD!**"

Having infinite expressions (meanings - *mana*), **MOHAMMED's ALLAH** is in a state of contemplating them fully at every moment!

The "ONENESS" *(tawhid)* principal in **Islam** that is the BELIEF SYSTEM notified by **Mohammed** *aleyhessalaam* that "THERE IS NO GOD TO WORSHIP, there is ONLY "**ALLAH**" who is AHAD, and therefore no GOD ever existed," is based on the fact that every person will be responsible for the result of his actions that are carried out through himself all through his lifetime.

Accordingly, the following signs in the **Koran** emphasize that every person will directly receive the return of his own deeds:

> *"And that man shall have nothing save only that for which he made effort."* (53:39)

> *"You are requited nothing save what you did"* (37:39)

> *"You are rewarded nothing except for your deeds."* (36:54)

> *"And for all there are degrees from what they do, that HU may pay them for their deeds and they shall not be wronged"* (46:19)

> *"Most surely you will taste the painful punishment-, this you will be responded nothing save what you did"* (37:39)

Since man will see only the return of practices he or she has done in this world as seen from the signs above, it must be the most urgent task for a man to make investigation about life beyond death and to understand what "**ALLAH**" means!

When **Mohammed** *aleyhessalaam* was asked the question, what is **ALLAH**, the answer was directly given by "**ALLAH**" in the **Chapter of ONENESS** in the **Koran**:

"**Say that: ALLAH is AHAD,**

ALLAH is SAMED,

LAMYALID and LAMYULAD,

And LAMYAKUN LAHU QUFUWAN, AHAD."

Let us first understand the deep rich meaning of these phrases in that Chapter that inform what **MOHAMMED**'s **ALLAH** is, and then start meditating on the results of their meanings.

"**ALLAH is AHAD**": It means **ALLAH** is the infinite and limitless (eternal) **ONE** who is unbroken and undivided into fragments or particles.

Now, let us try to comprehend this notification properly!

The "**AHAD**" who is the inseparable ONE unbroken, undivided into sections or particles (*zarra*), is either a limited and finite one —in this case, he dwells somewhere in the universe (!)— or is the limitless, infinite, unfragmented, whole ONE that in this case, only HU's OWN SELF alone, if I repeat, all and all **HU, only HU Itself alone exists!**

By reasoning and by understanding, it is groundless to claim any other thing's existence apart from what is informed through the name "**ALLAH**" who is "**AHAD!**"

Take a minute to consider this:

If it were for something apart from "**ALLAH**," that stands next to the one denoted by the name "**ALLAH**," where would the line between such a being and "**ALLAH**" take part? Where would you draw such a limiting line?

It is either that **there is the infinite and limitless WHOLE ONE**, without any additional separate being outside; or else, there is a limited and finite "GOD"(!) LOCALIZED somewhere inside or outside the universe!

The most important point to comprehend now is the concept of "LIMITLESSNESS - INFINITY."

So now, let us try to comprehend the conception of "limitlessness and infinity," not in terms of width, length and height but rather dimensionally.

In **ABSOLUTE REALITY**, the only **ONE** that exists is the infinite and eternal **ONE**, who is undivided and unbroken **WHOLE**, the **AHAD**!

ALLAH is AHAD, as there is nothing other than "**ALLAH**" neither in macro nor in micro plan, and there is nothing to be HU's counterpart, like or to match HU!

However, because of our dependence on our physical senses, we are fooled into thinking in which we mistakenly view the whole ONE existence to be composed of many separate parts and fragments. It must be understood that our brains' determination results from the condition of its intersectional sensory means.

However, if only a brain should not remain restricted in that very narrow range of its perception instruments' capability... If only it could understand and interpret all the perceptional phenomena evident to the five senses as **signs** and **samples** drawn out among countless sensory experiences in the cosmos...

If only after that he could sink into deep thought (*tafaqqur*) and discover what else is out there after these samples... If then he could sail to a dimensional journey into the structural depth of them... and meet with the cosmic self, the cosmic ESSENCE, and could even finally realize the "nonexistence" of his individual self beside this Universal Essence, in anyway...

This is the most significant point of the theme!

As to the second significant detail of the theme...

MOHAMMED's ALLAH is "AHAD" meaning the infinite, limitless ONE unfragmented into parts, and this state involves all aspects and all "DIMENSIONS." So in this case, where, in which dimension and at which starting point could a separate being presumed to exist beside HU's own being, limit ALLAH by a line and make a space for itself?

Where is the place for a second being, for a GOD that would be mentioned to exist apart from "ALLAH"?

Will it be inside or outside "**ALLAH?**"

As we have already stated, "**ALLAH**" is limitless and infinite.

Since "**ALLAH**" is limitless and infinite, it is an impossibility to consider HU within a CENTRAL CORE!

To recognize a center of something, it ought to have its boundaries, so that the point at which all its diameters meet may be considered as its center.

Yet, "**ALLAH**" has no limits.

If something does not come into measurement or a limit, then it cannot have a center! If something does not have a center, neither does it have a core nor an inside and an outside!

With reference to our current way of viewing the world through our five senses and our determination of substances based on our way of perceiving, we ascribe every object its external and internal parts, an inside and an outside sector. But it is senseless to talk about the core or the surface of something, an inside and an outside part of something that is not known by a center!

The same information is emphasized in the **Koran** as in the following sign:

> *"HU is the First (Awvalu) and the Last (Akhiru), the Visible (Zakhiru) and the Unseen (Baatin)"* (57:3)

This means: All that is known as **visible** and **unseen**, the **beginning** and the **last** is nothing other than "ḤU"! All those words in fact signify just a single being. That is, the distinction between visible and unseen does not really exist. They are not two separate things!

Call HU the Apparent (*Zakhir*) or the Unseen (*Batin*), the First or the Last as you like, but it all is still nothing other than HU indicated, no matter whichever word you employed.

Regardless of which word we employ, it is only HU that will be qualified or signified. The distinction between the visible and the unseen (i.e., physical and nonphysical) results from your five senses. You call as "visible" what you are capable of perceiving through your five senses and call the rest as "invisible" as they are unseen to you.

However, if you were in a condition of perceiving through more, for instance, six, seven or twelve sensory means, then your determination of all "the visible" and all "the unseen" would entirely alter! You would then likely call "visible" whatever you currently call "unseen," and "unseen" whatever you currently call "visible."

Since what is informed through the name "**ALLAH**" is the limitless and infinite **ONE**, HU is free from the limitations of such concepts as external and internal, and from concepts of *Zakhir* and *Batin*.

Of course, it cannot be mentioned for a being that defies any centers, any interiors and exteriors, any apparents and inwards, and any beginnings and ends, as it is free of all such conceptions and formations, to vanish at a particular place, so that a second separate existence should be found beyond such a point.

Here due to this, we realize that in every point ever perceived or imagined, all in all, merely **ALLAH** being **AHAD IS** and only **HU alone** is present with HU's ESSENCE *(Zhat)* and thence within all HU's properties and attributes.

If someone assumes the presence of a second being other than "**ALLAH**," —apart from "**ALLAH**," he is then entirely in a state of error resulting from an incapability of deep thinking! This state is called "POLYTHEISM" (*shirk* — ascribing a partner) in religious terminology!

Since "**ALLAH**" is "AHAD," no other being beside HU can be mentioned! Furthermore, HU cannot be referred to a time passage where HU would be considered in pieces. This is out of question, either.

"ALLAH is SAMED"

If we make a serious study, some of the deep meanings we find in the definition of the word "*SAMED*" are as follows: "That which has no gap, which is in perfect condition, is whole without holes and is impermeable; that which admits nothing in, nothing out". It means "solid," same as in that when we say "solid gold". In other words, mere, pure, the absolute!

As seen, all these statements essentially contribute and illuminate the content of the name **AHAD**.

If so, then how should one understand the meaning of "*LAMYALID*", simply meaning "HU DID NOT BEGET"...

Here is what should be understood at the first sight: "**ALLAH**" has never given birth to a second being from HU's own being!

In other way of saying, there is not an existence of a second separate being broken off **ALLAH**'s existence!

Because, **HU** is **AHAD**, the inseparable whole **ONE** undivided, unbroken and unfragmented into parts, elements or particles!

1- **HU** is limitless and infinite! Thus, it cannot be mentioned for HU to bring out a second being inside or outside Hu's self.

2- Since it is an impossibility to consider **HU** in parts or atoms because **HU** is **AHAD**, then there is not a second part which could be divided from **HU**!

Therefore, the presence of a second one broken off "**ALLAH**," which is meant to be begotten by **HU**, sharing **HU**'s qualities even, can never be considered!

Let us now understand "*LAMYULAD*," simply meaning, "**ALLAH WAS NOT BEGOTTEN.**"

At this point we are to understand that "**ALLAH** did not come into existence out of another being!"

How can one consider the One informed through the name "**ALLAH**" to be brought into being by another existence? "**ALLAH**" is AHAD, the ONE Alone who is infinite, limitless and unfragmented into parts!

To be able to think of an existence to beget "**ALLAH**", "**ALLAH**" needs once to be known by some directional or DIMENSIONAL limits, so that beyond such limits there would be mentioned a second existence to beget **HU**! And only then that such a second existence could beget "**ALLAH**" from itself!

"**ALLAH**" **is AHAD!**

Being AHAD means being limitless and infinite Whole undivided and unfragmented into parts.

Therefore, neither a vanishing point for **HU** nor an initiation of another existence beyond such a point can be considered.

Hence, a second being to make up, to BEGET "**ALLAH**" cannot be mentioned. Such a consideration is an impossibility!

This is what is meant by "*LAMYULAD*" as far as we could understand.

In conclusion, neither has "**ALLAH**" been begotten by another being, nor has HU beget another being such as a second separate being that came out of HU.

We have come to the final notification in this description:

"*LAMYAKUL-LA-HUU QUFUWAN 'AHAD*":

There is not an existence of another being after HU's macro or micro likeness; HU is matchless, peerless and is AHAD."

By the way, we should note a sign hereby: "*LAYSA KAMISLIHII SHAY'A*" (42:11) meaning, **"neither in macro nor in micro plan, there is nothing to be compared with HU."**

Meanwhile, we should also notify that significant point now in order to prevent some unfamiliar people with this subject, from falling into a mistake.

In some places of the **Koran**, such statements as "our god" and "your god" are cited occasionally. However, each is followed by an emphasis that "god" is "**ALLAH.**"

Well, could it be then suggested that "**ALLAH**" is a "god" *(ilah)*?

No, this can never be suggested!

Such kinds of statements are the clarifications made to the "**worshippers of a god.**"

They are being admonished that:

"Whatever they consider as "GOD" or whatever they call "GOD" does not exist at all, but it is ONLY "**ALLAH**" that exists in reality!" "Their god" and ours are just the same and one. Moreover, it is still "**ALLAH**," and is nothing other than "**ALLAH**."

Of course, by such statements, it is proposed to make people cleanse their conjectural "god" images and try to understand "**ALLAH**."

If the **Koran** is looked into carefully, it is noticed that such kinds of signs are addressed to polytheists *(mushrik)*, namely to those who assume the existence of a "GOD" despite the understanding of "**ALLAH**" and who worship a god.

Only then could their acceptance of a "god" translate into the understanding of "**ALLAH**."

Let us now consider honestly and with moderation!

Is **MOHAMMED**'s **ALLAH** introduced here the same as **GOD** that we either believe in or do not believe, but still name **ALLAH** as a **conditioning** in either case?

Could we use the word "GOD" or a concept of GOD to replace with *Hazrat* **MOHAMMED's** **"ALLAH"** and could a concept of "DEITY" be allowed instead? Will they be correct?

That is, what in reality has ever existed so far, that exists today and will exist tomorrow, IS the "*BAKI*" (deathless) "*WAJHAH*" (face) only, that will have been existing forever.

The only veil on "*WAJHAH*" is however, the name given to something, that this name is a veil put on later to a meaning of the *wajhah*. Yet the original being behind such a veil, and the meanings that make it up take their origins from the names of "**ALLAH**."

As a final word, it should be known for certain that no concept of a "GOD" out there, afar off man, that is, out of yourself, is meant by the concept "ALLAH" neither as introduced by *Hazrat* Mohammed nor in the Koran *al Karim*, but it is tried to make people comprehend the Limitless and ENDLESS ONE as the only Being ever existing by HU alone...

* * *

THERE IS NO "GOD!"
THERE IS "ALLAH!"

Zhikr, as we have commonly heard, is practiced in order to find favor in the eyes of <u>a "god-out-there"</u> by repeating his names!

Is it really for that?

In order to understand the reality about this theme, we must first of all realize "**what**" **and** "**who**" the "**mentioned being**" **is**...

Shall we practice *zhikr* (mentioning - meditation) of a "**GOD**" or of "**ALLAH?**" Most of the readers will naturally ask the following question now:

"—What difference does it make? Call him "GOD" or "**ALLAH!**" They are all the same! We, the Westerners have named him GOD! God is great!.."

No! God is not great! God is non-existent! Nonsense is any concept of a god!..

Who says it?.. It is said in the "***Deen-i* ISLAM**" and in its holy book **Koran** *al Karim* that explains **Islam**! **Rasul of ALLAH Mohammed Mustafa** *aleyhessalaam* says that!

We have tried to clarify the vital importance of the difference between the concept "**ALLAH**" and any concept of a "GOD," in great details in our books "**Mysteries of Human**" and "**ALLAH as Introduced by Mohammed**" which is printed nine times in English and we have tried to explain the "*Deen-i* ISLAM" based on the concept "**ALLAH**."

Nobody can comprehend what the "*Deen-i* ISLAM" is about and why it has ever come, unless one fully understands the difference in meaning between a concept of "god" and the name "ALLAH" signifies. Without understanding it, one keeps misinterpreting the matter of RELIGION! Furthermore, one can never understand the reason why the **practices** (prayers-*ibadat*) in the "*Deen-i* ISLAM*" have been **suggested** for human beings.

Therefore, we must, before all, fully comprehend the difference between what the word "**god**" refers to and the meaning that is denoted by the name "**ALLAH!**"

What does the name "**GOD**" tell us?

The word "**God**" is about a being afar-off yourself, myself, ourselves and away from the whole existence, who created the everything from outside, who observes us from outside and who, based on his judgement about ourselves, will either throw us into his Hell or admit us to his Paradise!..

Majority of humankind including all the religious authorities, who took the **religious** scriptures literally and could not go further beyond analogies, do believe in a "**god.**" They defend "**that god**" and endeavor to overrule people in the name of "**that god!**" The intellectuals and the people of reasoning do not believe in such a god, as they have conceived that there could not be such a thing. Therefore they do not give heed to the words of religious authorities.

Yet, the understanding of the "*Deen*" based on the concept "**ALLAH**" is a reality commonly cherished and experienced by all the **Sufis** and *Awliyah* (Saints)! Unfortunately, very few of men have been aware of this fact!..

According to the **Koran** *al Karim* that explains such a reality, "**ALLAH**" created the universe and everything that is perceived to be present, "within the Science (*ilm*) of Hu, through the Power (*qudrat*) of Hu and by means of the qualities that Beautiful Names (*asma-ul husna*) of Hu refer to." As a result of this, what we call the **laws of nature or the universal ORDER** is nothing other than the **ORDER** and the **SYSTEM** of "**ALLAH.**" By the same token, humans are in need of becoming aware of "**ALLAH**" **within their own ESSENCE** and turn toward their essence instead of worshipping a "**god**" outside themselves.

All of the *Awliyah* in all times, have sought to direct people toward an understanding of

"*Deen*" established on the concept "**ALLAH**" and toward a spiritual state of "**awe**" (*hashyat*) resulting from their understanding. On the other hand, the formalist religious authorities have always portrayed a "**god afar-off**" and have tried to make people get **scared** of him in order that they could establish their supremacy...

Neither the **Koran** and nor *Hazrat* **Mohammed** *aleyhessalaam* described a "**god-out-there**" who is watching us from outside, and who will judge by our deeds and make up his mind, and consequently throw us into his Hell or admit to his Paradise...

On the contrary, our holy **Book** and the **Rasul of ALLAH** inform us about "**ALLAH**" **being within ourselves, in our Essence who formed our own reality (***haqiqat***)!**

That's why such an act as gossiping about someone or misleading, cheating one, acting bad, or a wrongful seizure has in fact been done to "**ALLAH**" who is the **Truth** (*haqiqat*) of that person.

It is by the same reason that the **Rasul of ALLAH** notified: "**One has not been grateful for ALLAH until he is grateful for people!..**"

That is, it is "**ALLAH**" within the **Essence** (ultimate core) of anything perceived Whom you turn toward to thank, not an imagined god afar off you that you have created in your illusion. We cannot understand the perfection (superiority) of the "*Deen-i* **ISLAM**" up until we grasp this reality properly!

If so, may we ever name "**ALLAH**" as a male "**GOD?**"

It will be our next topic!

* * *

COULD "ALLAH" BE NAMED AS "GOD?"

A group of unaware people who pass judgements about the "**Religion**" based on their hearsay and false information, have been employing the word "**GOD**" instead of the name "**ALLAH,**" being unaware of the matter and thinking that these words both carry the same meaning, and also relating it with their patriotism according to their whims...

In the previous chapter, I have tried to make it clear that any concept that the word "**god**" refers to is completely different in meaning than what the name "**ALLAH**" refers to. These are two different words with completely different meanings.

Shall we now make it clear through a passage from the **Koran** Interpretation written by the excellent **interpreter Hamdi Yazir of Elmali** in 1940's, which is most comprehensive and detailed interpretation published in Turkish by the Religious Affairs Directorate. Let us see what he says in it:

*"The word **ALLAH** has never been applied to anything other than **ALLAH**, neither in proper form nor in common. Take the names such as "ilah" and "huda," for example; none of them is a proper noun as "**ALLAH**." They imply a concept of "god" (ilaah), "lord" (rabb) or "idol" (maabud). It has been said "gods"(alihatun) as the plural form of "god," "lords" (arbab) as of "lord," etc...Unlike, it has never been said "**ALLAH**S" and can never be said so. If we hear such a usage of words from someone, we conclude that he is ignorant and negligent. The noun "GOD" is not like this; you can even call false idols as "gods." Pagans (mushrikeen) even used to worship many gods. Some of them had so-and-so gods, others had so-and-so gods.*

*So, the common name GOD is not synonymous for the proper noun "**ALLAH**," and is not an equivalent for "**ALLAH**." "**God**" is a very common phrase! Therefore one should never translate the name "**ALLAH**" as "**GOD**."* (Vol. 1, p. 24-25)

One should never call "**ALLAH**" as "**god**," according to this excellent **Koran** Interpretation written in Turkish.

We must also take the following significant differences into consideration:

The word "god" is a common adjective, yet "**ALLAH**" is a proper noun for the **Unique Essence** (*zat*), out of Whose there is nothing independent in existence.

I mean, that is not a matter of mere languages or word pronunciation. There is an enormous difference between the meanings of these two words.

An understanding of a religion with a "**god**" or a concept of "**godliness**" is groundless and false!

The original "*Deen-i* **ISLAM**" in effect is fully based on the meaning denoted by the name "**ALLAH.**"

The statement *"la ilaha ill-Allah"* **means "there is no god, there is ALLAH alone."** In order to be an earnest Muslim, we must first distinct that difference in meaning properly.

If we limit our comprehension fixed with a concept of a "**god**," we suffer the detriment of the meaning the name "**ALLAH**" refers to, for it will consequently make us losers of the treasure of khaliphness (*khilafat*) mystery.

"God" is a being out-there, **afar-off yourself**, that is worshipped!

"**ALLAH**" is the Reality (*haqiqat*) **within your Essence**, Who is being served all along!

"God" is a bugaboo to be "frightened!"

"**ALLAH**" is the source of a "deep reverence," an "**awe**" (*hashyat*) for the people of insight, which is generated through comprehension of their **nothingness** beside the limitlessness and **infinity**.

"God" is a ruler and a judge afar-off, assumed to be out-there, which is sculpted in the minds of inefficient people according to their fancies.

"**ALLAH,**" unlike, is the **One and the only Absolute Being,** Who created the universes through Hu's own being and Who is being experienced along with Hu's Names (*asma*) at every particle, with none else to be compared onto Hu...

"God" is a fictitious balooney sculpted in people's minds in accordance with the humankind's perception, adorned and smartened up with various faculties and assumed as a possessor of people's imaginary ascriptions, at every age and in every community depending on the level of people's understanding.

"**ALLAH**" is *Ahad* (the Ultimate Whole), *Samed*, *Lamyalid* and *Lamyulad*.

Well, if so, can there be someone who is authorized to rule **IN THE NAME OF** "ALLAH" and **the *DEEN*?**

* * *

CANCEROUS THOUGHT OF GOD

Allah made me in the following way aware of the reason why it was extremely hard to make people of our day comprehend an important fact:

Most people agree that everything at our level of reality was made by a Creator and they name that Creator as "**GOD!**"

The "**god**" is constructed in the minds of people by way of conditioning (habituation), based on what they pick up from others in their surroundings -**not by questioning and reflecting**- as to the qualities and dimensions of such a "creator" so assumed to be outside of someone's being and of the whole existence.

From then onward, people embark on discussions with that version of "**god**" in their minds; however, they name their god as "**Allah,**" as "**Allah**" is the commonly used term in their community!

This is where the problem arises...

When you try to explain the qualities of the absolute being denoted by the name "**Allah**" to such a person, who does not even understand that the concept "god" is nonsense and no god exists, he then injects all those information into the god conception in his mind and makes his version of "god" grow into "Allah." But what should be done is that they should get rid of the idea of "god" entirely first and then try to **recognize the absolute reality denoted by the name "Allah."**

Here the injection of that information about "Allah" into the god in our minds makes this version of "god" or our opinions in our brains become cancerous in a way. **A version of god adorned with such qualities that in fact belongs to "Allah,"** grows day by day and spreads there... Therefore, our conception of "god" is gradually grown into "Allah" (Allahized). While the cancerous cells of the physical body ruin a person's life of the world, the cancerous god conception and the unawareness of the meaning denoted by the name "Allah," results in the ruin of a person's eternal life.

We urgently need to learn comprehensively what the concept of "GOD" and "godness" are and help the people of understanding around ourselves be aware of it!

If we seriously want to learn the being denoted by the name "ALLAH" as informed by **Mohammed** *aleyhessalaam* based on the **Koran** *al Karim* and to understand Hu, first of all we need to clean our consciousness from the assumption of a "**God**" **afar-off, out-there.**

How will we attain such a cleanness?

Truly by trying to read this universe that **Allah** created and we live in, along with the system that operates within it!

We will then be aware and understand that:

Everything that we are aware of is made by the knowingness (*ilm*)**, will and power of Allah.** Other than Hu's will, there is no one to will; neither can something be willed. Allah being *Haaqim,* makes every event adequately as it is based on a "*hiqmah,*" (wisdom) even if we find it untimely or inaccurate.

Furthermore, we must very well understand what the *murad* (that which is desired) of **Allah** is?

The Essence (*zhat*) whom the name "**Allah**" refers to and who has a disposal on the entire universes, exposes (brings into being) Hu's will at every moment in the form of existence. And there is not another being to question Hu from outside Hu's self.

One of the basic rules of the operation of the system Hu created is that "**always the powerful wins.**" The one who was given Hu's power continues to win until its encounter with the more powerful other. Because Hu's is the attribution of "**power**" (*qudrat*), not the "weakness" (*ajz*).

The **power** of each being arises from **his knowledge** —**insight** (*ilm*). Every being's possession of knowledge is at his mind's capacity. Each one assumes others as unwise, because each kind has a particular level of reasoning of its own. Each mind finds other minds as "**unwise**," the other being either outside or inside its own capacity.

Allah, however, bestows on each unit <u>what they deserve</u> (their sustenance) according to the purpose **for which they were created**, and so makes Hu's will realize. And this is exactly what we call as the <u>justice (*adalat*) of Allah</u>. It is therefore that, no injustice is in consideration in the past or in future in the universe in a real sense. Every individual receives at each moment **what it deserves as due with regard to the purpose for which it was created.**

So, if we want to purify our minds from the version of "**God**" that we have created in our imagination and then recognize the **Essence** (*zhat*) denoted by the name "**Allah**," we need to **READ** the universes and Hu's system **that Hu made existent from within Hu's own Existence...** That is the way to recognize the Maker by means of the works Hu made.

Only then the path for recognizing Allah should open up for us.

Otherwise, we will set off our eternal journey in such a state as mentioned in the **Koran**: "**Have you seen those who made gods of their own fancies?**"

IF "HU"
IS CONVERTED INTO "HE"

I would like to draw your attention in this chapter to a significant error that is in the English translations of religious publications as well as the **Koran**.

As known, the word "**HU**" in the **Koran** *al-Karim* is translated as "O" into Turkish. The pronoun "O" in our language denotes a third being and in this sense there is no difference between masculine, feminine and neuter forms. Regardless of their sexes or liveliness, only the word "O" is employed for the third beings no matter what.

Yet, there are three English equivalents of that Turkish pronoun "O" in translations. "He" for males, "she" for females and "it" for the rest.

We have also been using an incorrect phrase: "God-father!" This word has passed to our language from Christianity. They believe in a **God-afar-off in the sky**, a male god, who is assumed the father of Isa (Jesus) *aleyhessalaam*. Yet, as I have tried to explain throughout this book, what is informed through the name "**ALLAH**" is not a "male-father out-there!"

Let us try to think and realize our essence that is referred by saying "I."

Let us turn toward the core of a material object and **zoom** into it, descending to the dimensions of molecules - atoms - neutrons - neutrino - quarks and quanta, gradually. Let us then try our best to imagine the reality at the dimension of particle-waves. Here, all this is a dimensional ascendance or what is known as "*Miraj*" (Ascension).

The word "**HU**" in Arabic denotes a "dimensional-beyond" in a sense without quantity and quality!

Consider now the meaning that I've mentioned about "**HU**" and compare it with the meaning of the word "He," which denotes the third persons in the English language. Moreover, consider the conceptional confusion created by the alteration of the meaning of the word "**HU**" into what people are used to understand from "He!"

How correct can the truth be approached if the "**HU**" is understood as a god with a sex while it is intended to mean the "**point of ONENESS of universal dimensions**?"

How can an understanding of a "male/father god" recognized as the concrete behind the abstract, match with what is in reality free even from the descriptions based on the attributions of limitlessness and infinity?

What's more, this should particularly be understood that...

The universe known as <u>infinite</u> to us is an aspect only "<" made of a single "pin-point" (*nokta*) in a single "moment" (*an*)!

It is only an aspect "<" made up from a single "point" in the plane of infinity.

Everything that we refer with the terms "**universe**" and "**universes within the universe**" takes part in such an aspect –"<"- only.

Everything that takes part in that aspect "<" and a "pin-point" itself in which they all dwell in, is "HU's" creating in a single moment only within "HU's moments".

We are in a "universe" out of universes, that are created from a single "point" in only one single "moment" within countless "points" of countless "moments."

What is known as "*Insan-i Qamil*" (Universal Consciousness) or as "*Haqiqat-i Mohammedi*" is a being made of such a single "pin-point"!

"POINT," however, is nothing more than a "**witticism**" (*nukte*)!

"HU" is a "**wit**" at the sight of "points," while it is the Creator (*khaliq*) of countless "points"!

"HU" brings to existence all that was created from a "point" within HU's knowledge (*ilm*), with a <u>stuff of illusion</u>!

"HU" also denotes Who is *"GANI"* (transcendent) from all that was mentioned...

This is the truth (*haqiqat*) denoted by the noun "HU" that Muslims are required to realize?

Besides is the idea of a male-god-father denoted through the noun "He" in the translations of the **Koran**, in which the meaning of the noun "HU" is converted into "He."

It is extremely difficult for people to understand the *Deen-i* **Islam** through **Koran** translations that seems to refer to a god-afar-off.

If we desire to understand and consciously confirm the *Deen-i* **Islam**, we must first of all grasp the meanings that are specified through such words.

* * *

Chapter 3

DEATH

They who considered a God afar off, somewhere in space, also accepted that spirits are coming to physical bodies form up there on the side of that god out-there! They who are aware of "Allah," however, observed that spirit comes from the Haqq, that is the essence and the reality of a brain.

WHAT IS DEATH?
THE INNER FACE OF
"DEATH"

It is unfortunate that the reality of "**DEATH**" is not known in a true sense in our day, and DEATH is commonly assumed to be someone's "**ending**".

Actually, **without being life's ending**, DEATH is nothing more than a transition from the physical world to a world beyond the physical! It is just a **transformation**!

Right after a person's separation from his physical body through DEATH, his life goes on within a "**spirit**" — **hologramlike body of frequencies**— either in the grave or outside.

That is, DEATH is the continuation of life, beginning with the spirit body after the end of life with the physical body.

The **Koran** that informs the fundamentals of **Islam** explains "death" as follows:

"**Every SOUL will taste DEATH**!"

What we call DEATH is the transference into a life at a universe of frequencies within a spirit body after separating from the biological material body.

As the brain ceases to function, the bioelectric energy outspread to the body disconnects and the body loses the electromagnetic force that normally keeps the spirit tied to body. So the human SPIRIT is released to a new life independent from the physical body. Such an event is what is meant by DEATH.

All the activities realized through the brain of a person throughout his lifetime are stored in his spirit, i.e., hologramlike body of frequencies, like the waves of sound and vision. Therefore, the spiritual dimension is directly accessed without any change noticed of life on dying. The person continues his life in a form of SPIRIT the same way as he was within his physical body!

There is one difference however: Although he is still completely alive and conscious (aware) as before, he cannot conduct his physical body any more! Similar to a permanent vegetative state (PVS) patient (the state of being permanent vegetable) [he is alive and aware]! He can observe everything going on outside, can hear and sense them, but he cannot communicate or respond in any way to his physical surroundings in the outside world.

Following is a saying of **Mohammed** *aleyhessalaam* about death as the great Islamic Scholar and Sufi Ibrahim Hakki Erzurumi recounts it in his book entitled "*Marifatname* (Book of Gnosis):"

"The deceased (one who tasted death) knows those who washed his body, who shrouded the corpse, who performed the funeral service for him, who attended his funeral procession, who descended the corpse into the grave and who prompted over his grave! "

"Do not cry out by slapping your cheeks and tearing your clothes beside the deceased for he is tortured by your wailing!" This shows that he will be seeing and feeling troubled of the others' emotional states.

I want to draw your attention to the following saying of *RasulAllah*, that will make us clearly comprehend that, even though someone in grave —who has experienced his death, — has lost his tie with his physical body, he will still be living on in an aware and conscious state within his "spirit" and besides he will be hearing the addressing from outside.

As Talha* *radhi'allahu ahn* narrated:

"On the day of the battle of *Badr*, **RasulAllah** (peace and blessings be upon him) ordered that the twenty four corpses from the *Quraish* tribe should be picked up altogether.

---

* Likewise Talha, all these names refer to Mohammed's *aleyhessalaam* friends who narrated some of his hadithes and his sunna.

They were then thrown into a pit among the ditches of *Badr*; so, had more dirt added to it."

When a victory was gained, **RasulAllah** used to take up temporary quarters in the open fields gained from the enemy tribes each time for three days. As it was the third day of the battle of *Badr*, he ordered his camel to be brought. Food for the road was put upon the load.

As **RasulAllah** rode on, the companions followed him. Meanwhile they talked among themselves that **RasulAllah** was probably going for a purpose.

At last, **RasulAllah** stopped by a ditch where the killed had been thrown, and then called them by the name of their fathers:

"O, Aba Jahil Ibn-i Hisham! O, Utbe Ibn-i Rabia, O, So-and-so!! . . . Would not you be joyful now if you believed and obeyed "ALLAH" and HU's Rasul? The Killed! We have indeed found the victory that our Lord promised us. Have you, too, found the victory that your Lord promised you, indeed?"

On hearing him speak, Omar *r.a.* asked:

"O **RasulAllah**! How do you address people already cadaverous?"

RasulAllah replied:

"I swear by Whom in Whose hands Mohammed's soul is that you are no better than they at hearing what I say!"

In this event recounted in *Bukhari* [*], **RasulAllah** corrects a great misunderstanding by an occasion.

No *hadith* can be better to correct such a false belief that "men are laid into their graves being as dead and they are raised to life later again on the Day of Resurrection (*qiyamat*)."

In fact, men are put into grave in an aware, conscious and an alive state same as in our current state of life, and they hear the addressing from outside as easily as if they are outside.

Othman bin Afwan[†] *r.a.* who is the third *khaliph* to **RasulAllah**, used to shed tears until his beard got wet if he stood by a grave. He was asked once:

"You do not cry when remembering heaven and hell, but why do you shed tears because of the fear of the grave?"

Othman answered:

"As I have heard from **RasulAllah**, the grave is certainly the first of stations in the next world! If a person is freed from there, it will be easier to be released from the others to come. If he fails to become free from there, the others to come will then be more fierce!"

Othman then continued:

---

[*] Bukhari, one of the six well-known books of hadithes.
[†] Othman, a known Islamic figure, the third of the four khaliphes to Mohammed *aleyhessalaam*.

RasulAllah said that: "**I have never seen a TERRIBLE sight worse than that in a grave!**"

Standing by the grave of Sadd bin Muaz who was a leading Islamic figure and martyr for the **Islam** (*shahid*), *RasulAllah* (*salla'llahu aleyhe wasallam*) once said:

"**Such a distinguished servant was he that heaven trembled and its doors were opened for him and thousands of angels came on earth. Even he felt so squeezed into the grave that his bones almost crackled!**

If it were possible to escape from the torment of the grave and the afflictions after death, it would first have been bestowed on Sadd! He was immediately delivered from such afflictions owing just to the spiritual state he had reached; that is all!"

Take a minute to consider this! If men were not in an alive state, i.e., conscious in their graves, would such a torment ever be under consideration?

It was once asked to *Hazrat* Nabi:

"O *RasulAllah*! Who is the most aware and conscious among the believers?"

He answered:

"**Those who most often remember what befalls a man on death and who prepare themselves doing their best for such a life beyond death. They are the wisest, the most conscious and aware ones.**"

In another statement he noted that:

"The most conscious and the most farther-sighted man is he who makes himself (his soul) subject to divine orders and who deals with the deeds that will bring benefit after death. Weak is he who remains dependent on his own (selfish) desires and then expects favor from ALLAH!"

Ibn Masud who was among the companions (*ashab*) of **RasulAllah**, tells the following about the torment in grave:

"As I have heard from **RasulAllah**:

"Sinners will surely be exposed to the punishment (*azab*) of the grave; the beasts even have a sense of hearing their cries."

Narrated Abu Said al Khudri:

RasulAllah (*salla'llahu aleyhe wasallam*) notified:

"The unbeliever is obsessed by ninety nine monsters in his grave, each biting and stinging him until Doomsday. If any one of them had ever breathed over the earth, no grass would ever be able to grow then!"

Narrated Ibn Omar *radhi'allahu ahn*: **RasulAllah** notified:

"When anyone of you dies, he is shown his place both by day and night. If he is one of the people of paradise; he is shown his place in it, and if he is from the people of Hell-Fire, he is shown his place there-in.

Then it is said to him: 'This is your place till ALLAH will resurrect (*baa'th*) you on the Day of Resurrection!"

Now let us also pay attention to another point that is a sentence we recite in *Amantu*:

"*Wal baa'th u bad'al MAWT*" meaning "and [I believe] to revive right after (as a consequence of) DEATH"

Examine this carefully!

We do not say: "*Wal baa'thu bad'al KIYAMAT* (DOOMSDAY)."

It is that, the event implied by the word "*baa'th*" is not one after DOOMSDAY, but that after **TASTING DEATH**!

In this world, a person lives with his known physical body along with the spirit body constructed by his physical brain.

In parallel, great **Islam** scholar (*alim*) and Sufi (*mutasawwuf*) **Imam Ghazali** tells the following in the explanation of the name AL-BAIS in his book entitled "The Interpretation of *Asma Al-Husna*":

"*Most people are taken in by false conjectures and vague imaginings regarding this fact, the upshot of which is their imagining death to be mere absence, non-existence, or that the "baa'th" brings forth something new in the wake of this absence, as in the first creation.*

Before all, their presumption that death is non-existence is a mistake, as is their opinion that the second revival is like the first one.

Concerning their belief that death is non-existence, it is groundless. Indeed, the grave is either one of the pits of the fires of Hell, or a garden out of the gardens of Paradise.

Interior vision has guided the masters of intellectual perception to the fact that man was created for eternity and that there is no way for him to become non-existent.

Of course, there are times his tie with his corpse is cut off when it is said "he is dead"; or other times his tie may return, and it is said "he has enlivened, he has come to life."

Now, concerning their hypothesis that the resurrection is something like the first coming-to-be, that is not sound, they are wrong in their assumption, for the "resurrection" refers to another sort of creation quite unrelated to the first coming to life.

To tell the truth, human beings undergo a number of revivals, not only two."

* * *

On tasting death, human spirit is released from the physical body, so the life goes on within spirit, which experienced death, in a grave until Doomsday.

Far later it is once more revived (*baa'th*) on the base of its current (today's) characteristics during the term when the earth is corrupted in the heat of the Sun; which is known as "Doomsday!"

And ultimately all those bodies are formed by *baa'th* for the final time in accordance with the environment they reach.

Are we going to have our current awareness, perceptional- comprehensional mechanism in grave, also?

Abdullah bin Omar told about this point.

During a talk with **RasulAllah** about two angels known as *Munker* and *Nakir* who examine people in their graves, Hz. **Omar** asked:

"O **RasulAllah**! Are we going to be awake in the grave?"

"Of course. The same as you are now!"

What happens to the person who has tasted death, who is lucid, conscious but his physical body left out of order.

Shall we learn this from Anas *radhi'allahu ahn*:

"**RasulAllah** (*salla'llahu aleyhe wasallam*) said:

When a servant is laid in his grave and his companions return, he even hears their

footsteps leaving his grave. As they get away, two angels come up to him, make him sit up and then ask:

'What did you used to say about this man named Mohammed?'

If he is a faithful believer, he will answer:

'I bear witness that Mohammed is the servant of ALLAH and HU's Messenger.'

On his answer, it will be said to him:

'Have a look at your place in the Hell-Fire! ALLAH has replaced it for you with a place in Paradise.'"

RasulAllah added: He will then see his places both in Paradise and in Hell.

But if he is a non-believer or a hypocrite, (a Muslim by name,) he will answer:

'I do not have a certain idea. . . nothing more than what the people used to say!'

It will be said to him:

'Neither did you know nor take the guidance!'

Then he will be beaten by a mallet, and he will send such a cry that will be heard by whatever near to him except human beings and jinni!" (*Bukhari*)

Let us finally note the following *hadith* to conclude the subject.

"The deceased, —the person who tasted death— is tortured for the wailing of his relatives over him."

Many more *hadithes* of **RaṣulAllah** concerning this issue are available in related *hadith* books where they can be further studied.

As a brief conclusion from all:

Human beings NEVER DIE, BUT TASTE DEATH; so his dimension of life changes.

On tasting death, the person loses his tie with his physical body and goes on living from then onward within his hologramlike body of frequencies, i.e., his '**spirit**".

Therefore, awake is everybody when they are put into grave.

And they keep on living there in an aware and conscious state until the Resurrection day, when each person takes over a new body suitable to the conditions of that term.

* * *

We shall briefly mention now what else is undergone **after death is experienced**.

When DEATH is experienced, the person's perception of the external world still continues for some more time. Just the same as though he had been living within his biological body, he follows what is going on around himself, hears people's conversations and their wailing.

During that period he feels as if a patient in permanent vegetative state. He observes all events from outside, however he cannot communicate any response to the outside world.

By then, the time for the corpse's bathing comes.

As for the reason for washing the dead corpse...

The wisdom in bathing the corpse, as far as we could make it out, is to provide the body with a bioelectrical reinforcement by way of osmosis, while its cellular life still continues. As a consequence, the person may carry on his contact, though in an unshared way, with the world for some more time where he was moving about in a while ago with his physical body.

The dimension of life that begins at the time of DEATH is TASTED and continues till the Resurrection day is known as the universe of *BARZAKH* (Isthmus).

The life beginning by death is divided into three phases:

A. Life in a grave,

B. Life in the world of grave,

C. Life in the Isthmus (*Barzakh*).

A. **Life in a Grave**. This is the stage entered upon by someone's *baa'th* with his hologramlike body of frequencies —his spiritual body— after his tasting death, and it lasts as long as someone's life in grave continues perceiving his physical environment.

During that stage he continues perceiving everything that happens around himself both prior to his burial into grave and thereafter.

This transitional stage resembles that of our states in our beds before we sleep.

Prior to falling asleep, one lies in his bed in an aware state for some time, being aware of his surrounding, feeling how soft or hard the bed he lies on is. Similar to this one, someone in grave at this first stage perceives everything inside and outside the grave, as he is still alive there.

Just like a person who is about to sleep in bed, is aware of his environment while meantime falling asleep into a world of dreams in a half asleep state, someone at this first stage perceives the occurrences inside as well as outside the physical grave. Subsequent to this he enters for his journey into HIS OWN WORLD of GRAVE.

At the same time, two angels come up as informed in the *Deen-i* **Islam** and ask three questions that "**Who is your Lord?**", "**Who is your Nabi?**" and "**What is your Book?**"

PAY ATTENTION!

There is no question in GRAVE concerning someone's sect, order (*mazhab*) or cult (*tariqat*)! Never an *imam* of any cult nor any sect is discussed there!

THOSE WHO THINK THAT THOSE SORTS OF QUESTIONS WILL BE ASKED IN GRAVE ARE UNFAMILIAR WITH THE *DEEN*. Neither in the **Koran** nor in any of **Mohammed**'s *aleyhessalaam hadithes* is there an instruction showing that something about a cult or a sect will be asked in grave!

The sects and the other organizations were established long after *Hazrat* **Mohammed**'s *aleyhessalaam* transition into the universe of *Barzakh*. . . that such things do not serve in the universe of *Barzakh*, they are never mentioned there!

Subsequent to that examination comes the transition of the deceased into either his world of grave or into the universe of *Barzakh*.

What is the difference between the "**world of grave**" and the "**universe of *Barzakh***"?

B. **Life in the World of Grave**. In this stage, a person in grave resembles that of a man who is completely asleep in the world of dreams being unaware of his entrance to the world of dreams, and he continues to live his life as though still in his waking life.

Just like we experience our actual lifetimes in this world as if our only life, the person who has entered for his life in the world of grave experiences his new dimension of life the same way as his only life there. In the subsequent course, he either lives pleasing dreams of Heaven (*jannat*), enjoying himself peacefully, which is known as the "**heaven in the grave**," or lives in the nightmare kinds of frightening dreams of Hell among severe tortures and torments, **"the Hell-fire in the grave."** That phase keeps on the same way until Doomsday.

This is a person's life in his world of grave during his stay in a grave.

The following *hadith-i shariff* of our *Nabi* instructs that state:

"The grave of a human is either a garden out of the gardens of Paradise (*jannat*), or a hole out of the holes of Hell."

Besides that there is a life in the universe of *Barzakh*.

C. **World of *Barzakh* Life**. This is the dimension of life which is experienced by the martyrs (*shahid*) who have died on the path to **"ALLAH"** *fiysabiilAllah*, *Anbiya*, Rasuls and *awliyaullah* who have been known, if so mentioned, have **died before death** actually came to them. There they move freely within their **"spirit bodies"** as being liberated from the limitations of the grave life.

In the life of *BARZAKH*: Martyrs (*shehids*), Friends of **ALLAH** (*awliyaullah*) and Rasuls are able to move, to travel and make communication freely with each other owing to their status.

Besides, there is a hierarchy in the *Barzakh* life; and executives there in that hierarchy.

Further information is available in our book entitled "MYSTERIES OF HUMAN," under the title "*Rejal-i Ghaib*" (Spiritual Masters of the Unknown).

Out of those in the *Barzakh* life, a group of *awliya* who have reached the spiritual state of "*fatih*" during their lives in this world, can communicate with the ones in this world. However those *awliyaullah* who have reached the spiritual state of "*qashif*" but who have not attained "*fatih*" cannot get in direct communication with those in the world though they are completely free in their universe.

We have given further information about the spiritual states of "*qashif* and *fatih* " in our book "DUA and ZHIKR."

Each person continues his life after the EXPERIENCE OF DEATH either within his own world of grave or in the *Barzakh* as his spiritual station (*martaba*) allows him.

Such a life awaits every one of us!

Anyone can check out this information and see the truth of our explanations in related sources and places as he wishes.

* * *

WERE OUR "SPIRITS" CREATED IN THE PAST?

Now, I would like to clarify another significant misunderstanding...

"**Were human spirits created somewhere in the eternal past and then are they sent down to earth one by one?**" Does the "**Deen**" give that information?

Certainly not!

Human spirits were not created in the past, at the beginning (*azal*) and they are not being sent down to the earth into physical bodies periodically, one after another. On the contrary, each spirit is constructed by the brain of each individual on the 120th day in mother's womb **with an angelic influence that manifests as the power of "ALLAH" from within the essence of an embryo.**

The Chapter of Heights (*Sura A'raaf*) in the **Koran** gives us the following information in the sign 172:

"**And when your Lord brought forth from the Children of Adam, from their <u>loins,</u> their** seed, and made them testify of themselves, saying:

-Am I not your Lord? (*A-lastu bi-Rabbikum?*)

They said: Yes, verily. We testify. That was lest you should say at the Day of Judgment: Lo! of this we were unaware!"

By reason of failing to discern the essential fact that is cited in this sign, some twisted translations and completely unrelated renderings have been suggested for it; and having been adorned with many fallacious stories, those misinterpretations have finally reached to our day as a **common baseless (deceptive) acceptance**...

Briefly mentioning today's mistaken and groundless common acceptance: **"ALLAH created the spirits of all possible people to be born in this world collectively in a different location and asked them there, "— Am I not your Lord?" And people's spirits gave answer there as it were, saying, "—Yes, you are our Lord!.."**

What's more, it is assumed that those spirits descend one after another from there to earth and enter into physical bodies during their growth in mothers' wombs, afterwards; and they also go back from there to that realm later again.

Furthermore, in the opinion of some inconsiderate and narrow minded people

with a lack of deep and comprehensive information, those spirits come back to the world from there over again in order to reach perfection. And, they call that a "reincarnation" implying a return to this world by reentering into a different physical body.

An additional story is also invented under the name *"bezmi elest"* in association with such a misunderstanding. Supposedly, those who met and felt affectionate with each other there, also met here in this world; those who used to love each other there also loved each other here; and those who disliked each other there disliked each other here as well!...

Now, let us first sum up the reality about that matter and then offer our evidence respectively.

Allahualem, here is the meaning that the mentioned sign implies:

According to the rule (*hukm*) that "**ALLAH created human on an Islamic nature,**" **every individual is born after the genetic information transferred from father with a program of** "Islamic constitution" (*fitrat*)**, while someone was in a form of sperm yet at that time;** and it then passes through the following stages...

The statement "**from their loins, their seed, (***zurriyyah***)**" indicates and emphasizes the availability of that information of "**Islamic disposition**" (*fitrat*) transferred genetically through sperm. That is, human beings have been endowed with a natural faculty of being aware of their Lord, while yet in a form of sperm —when their seed was brought from their loins.

In point of fact, the embryo endowed with that genetic information, begins constructing its afterlife realm body known as "SPIRIT" on the 120th day in mother's womb, in form of frequencies produced by brain, through the agency of an angelic influence upcoming dimensionally from within its own core, its essence... And the "spirit" stores all the information produced in the form of waves as the outcome of all mental functions. **Therefore, the theory that a spirit consciously came from a different location and entered into a physical body is completely invalid.**

If we seriously consider the above verses of the **Koran**, which is tried to be imposed as an indication of existence of a "separate world of spirits" created prior to the earthly lifetimes at a different location, we realize that nothing but "**the seeds from the loins of Children of Adam**" is mentioned of there. The seeds and "loins" are issues of our physical world dimension we are currently in, not of the spiritual realm. Water of loins is semen and is in consideration in the world of sperm.

We have given further information about that matter in our book entitled "**WHAT MOHAMMED READ.**" You might also find more information confirming our explanations in the

4th volume, page 2324 of the **Koran** Interpretation written in Turkish by **Hamdi Yazir of Elmali**. You may see also a contemporary Interpretation of the Glorious **Koran** by Mr. Suleyman Ates.

Imam Ghazali tells the following in his book *"Rawdhatu-t Taalebiin"* about this matter: "**... Because, the spirit of our Master RasulAllah had not been created and did not exist before he was given birth by his mother!**"

Since a spirits is not something entering a body from outside, could its reentrance into another bodies over and over again repeatedly after its detachment (death), be possible?..

Let us continue in the next chapter...

* * *

WILL YOU RETURN TO THIS WORLD ONCE AGAIN?

The familiar idea of reincarnation, which is actually based on Hindu philosophy of thousand of years past, is currently being reintroduced as if it were a new revelation. This idea is also referred to as "*TANASUH*" and is based on a view that some time after the transition into the dimension of life with a spirit body from the life of physical body through death, the deceased will return to the earth through entering into a different physical body.

What is more, this idea is tried to be linked with some signs in the Koran as if it were accepted by the *Deen* of Islam and through twisting some interpretations to fit their objective it is tried to make believers swallow it as an Islamic fact.

It is an unavoidable truth that life will go on in the form of a different body right after the event of death. Since the entire science world has recognized the precision of the principle that "matter can neither be created nor destroyed (something that exists can never be absent)", then neither can an absence for your soul, your consciousness be considered! This scientific fact clearly assures the continuity of human consciousness, soul without any interruption after the event of death.

As a person's consciousness, that is his "soul", exists and lives on with a biological body at our current level of existence, and as this self will never be destroyed once it exists, then it is obvious that life will continue with a body within the framework of its environment following death.

Referring to the facts that the dimension of existence beyond the physical is a dimension of waves and frequencies, and human brain converts the bioelectric energy into a "substance of frequencies," then human will necessarily exist as a "body of micro frequencies" in the afterlife and live on within the framework of such micro frequency dimension.

It is known with certainty that each human exists with a biological body in this world of substance, the up-atomic plane, and the brain constructs a substance of frequencies by converting the bioelectric energy of his mental activity into frequencies. So in this case, is it possible for a human to return to this world after his transition into the afterlife realm of micro frequency-dimension through death?

REINCARNATION, the view of returning to this world through rebirth after our departure, can only be accepted by people of superficial approach whose point of start is a concept of

GOD and who cannot understand and realize the SYSTEM of life that ISLAM informs, as well as the concept of "ALLAH" and the natural consequence of understanding this concept!

It is completely baseless as a view to expect "a spirit to reenter a physical body" that is an illusion of those who cannot comprehend the difference between a "GOD" and "ALLAH" as explained in the *Deen-i* ISLAM and in the KORAN and who are unaware of the concept "ALLAH" as well as the operation of the universal System that is rooted in the content of this concept. Why is it baseless? We will try to explain the answer to you in this booklet.

We must know it before all that neither the spirits of people have been created collectively in an unknown place by a GOD standing somewhere above, once upon a time; nor are there any spirits to be sent one by one to the world sometime gradually. Neither is there a GOD-out-there dwelling somewhere above, nor any spirits waiting for their turns to come down to this world. For that reason, it is never possible for a spirit to come from outside to enter a physical body.

Actually there are two dimensions that we can perceive. One is the up-atomic level that is recognized as the "physical universe," the other is the subatomic level, which is the dimension of frequencies known as "SPIRITUAL UNIVERSE."

Everything is on a journey in this universe, which starts from the level of pure energy-consciousness and goes into the dimension of frequencies, and continues toward the physical dimension of up-atomic level from there, and subsequently reaches again to the subatomic dimension of frequencies.

After the early formation of brain kernel at the up-atomic level, individual human consciousness and soul begin to be recorded onto a "body of frequencies", that is the person's spirit, by the physical body mechanism. Therefore, after the life of biological body ceases, the soul continues to live with a construct called as "spirit."

Every human, i.e., every human brain produces his own parallel form in frequencies, "his double of frequencies," and continues to live with this frequency double.

The main function of human brain is in fact to construct this luminous body of frequencies that maintains person's eternal life beyond death and to store his consciousness, that is all his mental functions, onto that frequency-body.

Every spirit, that is every micro frequency-body is constructed and loaded BY ITS OWN BRAIN ONLY. For this very reason, there is no possibility for a spirit to return to this world by rebirth and to continue living through reentering a biological construction. The process in life always advances forwards, and never backwards.

Therefore, the Koran has emphasized the impossibility of returning to this world in any case in a number of signs, and *Hazrat* Mohammed has given parallel notifications about the same matter.

Besides, some saints (*wali*) and Sufis (*mutasawwuf*) who are familiar with the mysterious aspects of this matter have also explained their thoughts by stating that "human spirits did not exist before humans were created," and that "the spirits came to being only after the physical constructions came to being."

As a matter of fact, one of the greatest Islam Scholars (*alim*) and Sufis (*Mutasawwuf*) Imam Ghazali, who lived approximately nine hundred years before our day, explains the following in his book *"Rawdhatu-t Talebiin,"* to discard that sophistry which assumes the creation of spirits prior to physical bodies:

"One who knows the actions of Allah Taala and how Hu brings to being the life forms and plants on earth through moving the heavens, the stars by the agency of HU's angels, will understand the likeness between Adam's (human-being) disposition in his own universe and the disposition of the Creator (Haliq Taala) in the greater universe, he will also understand the meaning in RasulAllah's notice that "ALLAH formed mankind in HU's own likeness."

If the meaning in RasulAllah's sayings that "I existed as a prophet even before the creation and I am the last earthly prophet" and "When I was a Prophet (Nabi), Adam was in between soil and water" is asked, although the spirits are created at the same time as physical bodies?

The truth is that there is no proof in any of these statements that spirits are "ancient," i.e., existed in the past prior to physical bodies. However, with respect to the visible aspect of the statement that "I existed first as a prophet in the creation," there is a possibility of proof that his reality came to being before his physical build. Its meaning pertaining to the non-visible is obvious. Rendering and interpreting it is also possible. However, those proofs do not apply to the visible. On the contrary, they are used to establish the interpretation of the visible.

As for the meaning of "Allah created spirits two thousands years before the corpses," the spirits mentioned here refer to the spirits of angels. Also the corpses here refer to the Throne, Qursi, Heavens, the constellations, and the body and build of universes such as air, water and earth.

As for the meaning of "I am the first of prophets in creation," the word creation here is "khalq" meaning the "ordainment" (taqdir). It does not imply an "ejad," meaning to construct and create.

Because, RASULALLAH aleyhessalaam HAD NOT BEEN CREATED AND DID NOT EXIST BEFORE HE WAS GIVEN BIRTH BY HIS MOTHER!

However, the reasons and realities are earlier in terms of ordainment but later in terms of creation. As a matter of fact Allah Taala ordains (taqdir) and forms the affairs according to HU's science (ilm) first in "lawh-i makhfoz."

If you have conceived two aspects of existence explained up to this point, you must have understood that the existence of RasulAllah is "earlier" than that of Adam, not in terms of the visible reality but of the existence in ordainment. Ghazali ended his words thus...

Yes, many *awliyah* such as Imam Ghazali and Abdulkadir Geylani who have been familiar with the truth of this matter, refuse the idea that spirits were created before bodies, and state that every person's spirit comes to being together with and produced by his body.

We have explained this subject more comprehensively in our book entitled SPIRIT-MAN-JINNI.

Summing up the matter, it should be mentioned now that: The substance known as "spirit" is person's "hologramlike body", which begins to form following the 120th day of pregnancy in the mother's womb and is sculpted actually by the person's brain. Every human brain sculpts its own "body of frequencies," "his spirit," while in this world and this "body of frequencies" maintains its life always forwards in the afterwards without any reversible action such as returning back to this world for another time.

The spiritualists who support the idea of people's reincarnation back to this world misinterpret (deviate the interpretation of) some verses of the Koran by twisting them according to their whims. Here is the true interpretation of those signs, that they try to twist the interpretation to fit their objective as a proof:

1. HOW CAN YOU COVER [THE TRUTH OF] ALLAH, SEEING THAT HU GAVE YOU LIFE WHEN YOU WERE JUST DEAD. HU WILL CAUSE YOU TO DIE AND RESTORE YOU TO LIFE AND THEN YOU WILL RETURN TO HU. (2:28)

2. YOU CAUSE THE NIGHT TO PASS INTO THE DAY, AND THE DAY INTO THE NIGHT; YOU BRING THE LIVING OUT OF THE DEAD AND YOU BRING THE DEAD OUT OF THE LIVING. YOU GIVE WITHOUT STINT TO WHOM YOU WILL. (3:27)

3. (Prophet Noah addressed to his tribe:) ALLAH HAS BROUGHT YOU FROM THE EARTH LIKE A PLANT. AND TO THE EARTH HU WILL RESTORE YOU. THEN HU WILL BRING YOU FORTH AFRESH. HU HAS MADE THE EARTH A VAST EXPANSE FOR YOU. THAT YOU MAY GO ABOUT THEREIN IN ITS SPACIOUS PATHS. (71:17,18,19,20)

These are the translation of a few signs, with which the reincarnationists try to affirm their objective in order to draw the Islamic communities to support them. When these signs are interpreted, it will be clearly seen how much they strive to divert the meanings.

The meaning of the first sign...

O human beings! How can you deny Allah, that is, cover the truth of Allah's existence? That when YOU WERE JUST DEAD, (that we have previously explained the death,) HU GAVE YOU LIFE, meaning HU enfolded you in a physical making before which you were not yet under the restrictions of the physical world; then HU WILL CAUSE YOU TO DIE, meaning he will detach you from your physical build with which you have been enfolded (disguised); and will save you from the restrictions of the physical world and HU will return your physical bodies into the earth where they originally came from. HU WILL RESTORE YOU TO LIFE AGAIN, that is, HU will enfold you within the physical making on earth again on the Day of Judgement following Doomsday (*qiyamat*) and will make you survive within a physical body. And finally you will be returned to HU, in other words, you will be disconnected from the physical restrictions permanently, without any other return to the physical world again and will REACH ALLAH...

* * *

As seen, if the sign is looked into as we have mentioned above, it will be seen that there is no statement that provides evidence that people come to and go from the world over and over again to undergo a perfection, or come and go countless numbers of times up until reaching a perfection.

If it were at all possible to come and go over and over again as they claim, this evidence would certainly be mentioned and made clear in this sign or in another.

As for the meaning of the second sign mentioned above:

YOU CAUSE THE NIGHT TO PASS INTO THE DAY, meaning you transform the night into a day; YOU CAUSE THE DAY TO PASS INTO THE NIGHT, meaning you turn the day into a night; that is, you never leave anything in one manner, you change it into the opposite. YOU BRING THE LIVING OUT OF THE DEAD: You bring into the physical world those that were not yet limited within the physical world, by putting them in flesh and bones, so that you make them exist on earth and this way you bring forth the living. Then, YOU BRING THE DEAD OUT OF THE LIVING, meaning you KILL those that appeared within a body enfolded in flesh and bones in this physical world, that are called the living, through releasing them from the limitations of the physical world.

You give without stint to whom you will.

As also seen in this sign, not to mention a reference, there is not even an implication that people go and come back to this world over and over again in order to undergo a perfection.

However, unfortunately, those people who have been seduced by some "jinni" and have fallen into a struggle of proving their claim right, deliberately deformed the interpretation of these signs according to their logic so as to receive support from them.

Actually if such people are examined, it will easily be seen that they have not got the least bit of information about neither Islam nor the Koran, at all.

As for the meaning of the third mentioned verse:

3. ALLAH HAS BROUGHT YOU FROM THE EARTH LIKE A PLANT, that is to say, ALLAH formed (*khalk*) Adam, your ancestor and the first ever human seen on earth, from the earth. HU composed his physical making from a number of component elements that are originally of the earth. AND TO THE EARTH HU WILL RESTORE YOU. It is that, you will be released of physical restrictions through detachment from your physical body, and so your body will return to the earth from where it came originally. THEN HU WILL BRING YOU FORTH AFRESH. That is, upon the coming of the Day of Judgement, your body will be created at once on the basis of your spiritual state as that in grave, without undergoing the same kind of circle gone through previously during your growth in this world, and through

putting your main substance in it, you will be brought afresh from the earth.

ALLAH HAS MADE THE EARTH A VAST EXPANSE FOR YOU. The earth exists in a form appropriate to live on within your physical build. SO THAT YOU MAY GO ABOUT THEREIN IN ITS SPACIOUS PATHS. So that you may travel to any place you will and go about and live there as you wish.

Besides, we shall also dwell on some deep meaning of these two words. In Sufi (*Tasawwufi*) terms, EARTH refers to the "MIND" (intellect-*aql*). Considered within this context, the above signs mean: ALLAH has given the "mind" as a vast area, so that you may move on and make progress in its expansive paths of thought which raise according to various ways of operation.

That is, human beings have been given a form capable of moving along various paths, and besides, the Koran shows "*sirat-i mustakim*" (the path on the right direction) on that ALLAH wishes him to make progress..."

I hope I could have explained how blank are the foundations, on which those who are obsessed by the *jinni*, and who assume that they can prove "reincarnation" based on the *Deen-i* Islam, try to build their ideas.

The following sign must be well understood; which emphasizes that the person who has detached from his biological body cannot return to this world once again:

"WHEN DEATH COMES TO EACH OF THEM, HE WILL SAY: "LORD! LET ME GO BACK. THAT I MAY DO GOOD DEEDS IN THE WORLD THAT I HAVE LEFT BEHIND!" NEVER! THESE ARE THE WORDS WHICH HE WILL SPEAK. BEHIND THEM THERE SHALL STAND A BARRIER (*BARZAKH*) TILL THE DAY OF RESURRECTION." (23:99/100)

RasulAllah has notified that "THERE IS NO ONE TO BE RETURNED AFTER HIS DEATH." (Yazir, Hak Dini: v.6, p.4197)

The 128th sign in the 6th *Sura* of the Koran indicates the fact about people's going under the influence of JINNI, knowingly or unknowingly:

"JINNI! YOU HAVE SEDUCED MANKIND BY A LARGE MAJORITY!"

In the Koran *al Karim*, there is one chapter and a number of signs about "JINNI". One who denies the "JINNI," will be among those who deny the truth.

The above sign is followed by:

"And their votaries among men will say: Lord, we have enjoyed each others company. But now we have reached the end of the appointed term, which You decreed for us. Allah will say: The fire shall be your home, and there you shall remain for ever save those Allah ordains otherwise..."

Even "IBLIS" who is known as SATAN, is from the jinni. This fact is made clear in the 50th sign of the Chapter of *Al Kahf*:

"THEY PROSTRATED THEMSELVES (BEFORE ADAM) EXCEPT IBLIS. BECAUSE HE WAS ONE OF THE JINNI..." (18:50)

The ultimate desire of the jinni is to deviate people from their belief and make them deny the Koran. Thus, giving baseless inspirations, they misguide people toward some ways of thinking away from Islam, such as Hindu belief. They make people lean on a belief in GOD by way of turning them away from the belief of ALLAH, and urge them toward assumptions opposite to the understanding of "unity" (*tawhid*).

IT IS NECESSARY for human beings to understand the "JINNI" better in order to protect themselves from their dangers and their influences as they are extremely serious mischief-makers for humans. Because, there is no Satan other than the jinni, against whom the Koran *al Karim* warns us so frequently!

The Koran states that the JINNI are made from "smokeless fire," that is, " subtler frequencies" (micro waves) and also made from "poisonous fire capable of penetrating pores," that is to say, they have a "radiant-like making (substance)." Their influence on humans is similar to our brains' interpreting the telepathic waves. That is why we are not able to determine how and from where their influences do come.

Finally we shall state the following:

If those of you who think he or she communicates with (channeled to) spirits, who is disturbed by the jinni, who believes in reincarnation, who thinks he or she is under the influence of witchcraft, or who feels various repression and strains over himself or herself, might learn by heart the following signs and recite them 300 to 500 times a day, they will see great benefits very soon. Here is the prayer given in the Sura *al Sad* sign 41, Sura *al Mu'minun* sign 97/98 and Sura *al Saffat* sign 7:

"*Rabbi anniy massaniyyash shaiytanu binusbiyn wa adhaba. Rabbi auwzu biqa min hamasatish shaiyateyney wa auwzu biqa rabbi an yakhdhurun. Wa khifzan min kulli shaiytanin marid.* "

* * *

Chapter 4

ISLAM

ISLAM is the **Deen** at the sight of "**ALLAH**".

(The **Koran**)

UNDERSTAND "ISLAM," NOT "MUSLIMISM"

There are enlightened people and enlightened -like ones in this world in our days...

There are intellectual people and intellectual-like ones in this world...

There are also shepherds along with sheep who long for being steered.

And... There is "**ISLAM**" and also, there is people's "**Muslimism!**"

Enlightened is the one who seeks, finds and knows the truth based on his own objective investigations from true sources. However, enlightened -like ones are those who take advantage of the enlightened ones depending on their capacity to understand and try to take the hat round (get the benefit) by selling them to their surroundings.

There are intellectual people in this world... They are free from their cocoons at a certain level, and they try to lead their lives under the guidance of reasonable scientific thought. Also there are intellectual-like ones who like the perspectives of intellectuals' and the way they live. They imitate the intellectuals and take great pains to look like them, trying to wear, eat, drink, speak and act socially like them!..

Enlightened-likes and intellectual-likes are like zircons shining like a diamond to the eyes of suburban people. Their gleam attracts those in the outskirts of towns. But they haven't seen and cannot tell the difference between zircons and diamonds. Therefore their goal is only zircons. They are ready to sacrifice nearly all they have so that they may be like them, yet they cannot even be "...-like" of them.

There are those who love to shepherd as a result of their constitutional (native -fatri) inclinations and endowment they were created with. They strive to govern and rule people, longing for physical or moral satisfaction. They form groups to rule, they issue orders, bring restrictions and prohibitions so that they may satisfy their **unrealized subconscious militarist desires**. Moreover, there are those who ardently want to be steered or to be a door servant; who prefer to cover up their weaknesses and feel peaceful, as they find safety and protection in such.

This is the way it is no matter wherever you are, whether in Turkey or elsewhere in the world!

Yet, **ALLAH** created human beings to be the **"most honored"** of all creation, to be Hu's own **khaliph** on earth! But who has a care in that?..

Yes, both **intellectual-likes** and **enlightened-likes** in like manner comment on the people's "**Muslimism**," that gets around on the tongue of steered-people and that contradicts with logic, reasoning and science in most ways; and stressing on the underdevelopment of the followers of the religion of Muslimism, compared to other world societies, they assume that they are attacking the "*Deen-i* ISLAM" in this way.

Since they are never aware and conscious of themselves to be not more than yet intellectual-LIKE or enlightened-LIKE ones, they do not know that the "*Deen-i* ISLAM" and "**Muslimism**" are far different concepts from each other. Neither do they know that one should not even touch the religious issues unless one is aware of such a difference.

In point of fact, they leave aside the diamond without recognizing it at all, because of their assumption that the zircon-value perspectives and opinions of those who are desirous either for shepherding or being shepherded, are the fundamental thought systems of the "*Deen-i* ISLAM".

What else could indeed be expected from such helpless ignorant who consider as the only reference, the melody in the limelight among those who are desirous for steering and who want to be steered!..

Assuming that it is the "*Deen-i* ISLAM," they judge the narrow minded people's

"**Muslimism,**" in which melodious recitation of a poem (*mawlud*) and celebration of holy **nights with candles** are regarded as religious practices (*ibadat*), head-scarf is regarded as if it were the primary requirement of becoming Muslim for women, and *Salaat* and fasting were believed to have been ordered to please the heart's desire of the sky god of SkyTurks!

They do not understand that their so-called holy(!) poems were only written by people, (as *Mawlud* by Suleiman Chelebi) and they have no relation with the **practices** that the **Koran** *al Karim* recommends to humans... They cannot tell that litting candles on graves has no relation with the "**Deen,**" and only definite nights such as *Miraaj*, *Baraat*, *Qaadir* hide valuable hours within. They have not even heard that there is no such religious festives as Muslim festive of Sugar and Sacrifices, they are only the *Eids of Fitr* and *Hajj*! They have not comprehended that such **practices** mentioned in the **Koran** *al Karim* as *Salaat*, fasting and *Hajj* (Pilgrimage) have been offered not aimed at **pleasing the heart desire of a god in the sky,** but were recommended **for constructing people's future for their own salvation...**

The "**Deen-i ISLAM**" is a **time-free universal System and Order at the sight of ALLAH. It is the origin and the main, and is not distorted by time.** The **Koran** tells this!

However, "**Muslimism**" is people's interpretation of the "**Deen-i ISLAM**" within the framework of their personal capacity, their conditioning, the traditions and customs in their social environment and the restrictions brought about by their shepherds.

Now understand that the "*Deen-i* ISLAM" is not bounded by interpretations! Try to recognize the Origin! Get rid of the "**Muslimism,**" consider the "*Deen-i* Islam!"

Let us dwell on their difference in the next chapter...

* * *

THE DIFFERENCE BETWEEN "MUSLIMISM" AND THE "*DEEN-I* ISLAM"

In our days, either because of our ignorance in terminology or because of our conditioning to accept some information without any thinking and any inquiry of basis in fact, we are not aware of the extremely important difference between "**Muslimism**" and the "*Deen-i* ISLAM" and therefore we fall into serious misunderstandings. These two are far different concepts.

My primary goal in all these writings, is to make two very significant facts known:

1. The most significant difference in meaning between a concept of "**God**" and the name "**ALLAH**."

2. The most important difference in meaning between the words of "**Muslimism**" and the "*Deen-i* Islam."

I have already explained the first one in my previous chapters. Those of you who would like to learn more about it in details may apply to our book entitled "**Mohammed's ALLAH,**" that is published thirteen times in Turkish and nine times in English. We have also its German, French and Russian translations just for the interest of those who would like to distribute abroad. Our free booklets can be requested from Kitsan Publishing House at the fax number: ++90.212.5115144

As far as the difference between "**Muslimism**" and the "*Deen-i* ISLAM" is concerned...

The "*Deen-i* ISLAM" is a **time-free universal SYSTEM and ORDER at the sight of** "**ALLAH.**" "**ALLAH**" has informed to the humanity that time-free universal **SYSTEM** and **ORDER** that HU created, through the words of **Hu's Rasul**. The goal is to make people realize the current and eternal facts beyond daily anxieties and desires, in order to both recognize "**ALLAH**" as their own truth; and at the same time construct their eternal lives by means of the **qualities of ALLAH**, that are unfolded (expressed) from within themselves.

A "**Muslim**" follows the RasulAllah's instructions **to the extent of his understanding**.

"**Muslimism**" is people's overall acceptance concerning their understanding and interpretations of the **RasulAllah's** explanations **depending on their personal capacity**. This involves all Muslims.

Each of us can have our personal interpretation about the "*Deen*" based on our experience, understanding, insight, environment of growth and education, our ability and capacity, the capacities of people who had role in our development and finally the social conditionings and judgements of the environment of our growth and education. All they form up our "**Muslimism.**"

The "*Deen-i* ISLAM" is not attributional or relative; and it does not vary with reference to someone's personal perception. It is absolute, firm and invariable. This **SYSTEM** and **ORDER** is also called as "*SunnatAllah*" in the **Koran** *al Karim*.

No matter who one is and whatever spiritual state he shares, everyone can realize this **SYSTEM** as far as he could understand it. Everything ranging from the formation and existence of galactic masses, down to the consciousness at the level of genes takes part and operates within this "**SYSTEM**". No doubt, **for a rational person, man is not a missing independent ring of a chain that extends from genes to galaxies**. It is not, for insightful people, not for people who are detached from materialistic understanding and have a scientific consideration.

Unfortunately, a great majority of Muslims is born and raised under a **religion of Muslimism** and do not find out and neither become aware that there were the "**Deen-i** ISLAM" also **outside their cocoons.**

And then it is asked: "If the **Koran** were such a great book, why then do the Muslims in the social world form some undeveloped societies?"

Let me ask, how further would one go on with that religion of "**Muslimism**" that was replaced with the "**Deen-i** ISLAM" after being extremely narrowed down and turned into a "**cocoon**" and that was accepted as a religion of formality and worship in hope for some favor from a **sky god-afar-off?**

Where would one ever reach by associating so many sagas, superstitions, nonsense stories and countless illogicality with the *Deen* itself, rather than trying to understand the Book of **ALLAH?**

By reading and repeating the books of a path leader, perhaps without understanding them at all, one will never get out of the cocoon of the **religion of** "**Muslimism**" and get at the "*Deen-i* Islam!"

You need to construct your own understanding individually by means of exchanging ideas with others. Because, you will pass to the Hereafter (*akhirat*) on your own and will reckon for yourself there.

Those who let people read the books only of their personal path and forbid the rest, are the waylayers of the "*Deen-i* Islam," even though they might seem as the *Effendis* of the **"Religion of Muslimism."**

You need to construct your own understanding upon reading all the leading people of spiritual consciousness and thought — from **Imam Ghazali,** to **Shahi Nakshibandy,** from **Abdulkadir Geylani** to **Hadji Bektashi Wali,** from **Mewlana** to **Said Nursi** and see how they each understood the *"Deen-i* Islam," so that you may get away from imitation and from being shepherded, in order to be introduced to the *"Deen-i* **ISLAM"** and reach the **"Truth"** (*haqiqat*)!

There is no other way of liberation for all people including Muslims than to reconsider the *Deen-i* **Islam,"** with an approach that is purified from the **materialistic point of view.**

* * *

Chapter 5

RASUL

Verily a Rasul came to you from
within (*anfus*), who is Aziz!…
(*The **Koran***)

"READING" RASULALLAH

While it is so much important to "**read**" the **Koran** *al Karim*...

Do you think it is at all behind it to "**read**" the **Rasul of Allah** who brought us face to face with the **Koran** *al Karim*?.. How far and to what end do you think the "**Book**" could be "**read**" without "**reading**" the **Rasul of Allah** who communicated It to us?

People including Muslims in general are not concerned about "**reading**" **RasulAllah**, at all!

In the eyes of that **dull-witted** majority...

Hazrat **Mohammed** *aleyhessalaam* were, as if, a postman on earth chosen for communicating the commandments of a god who sits on the Sirius star and sends commandments down from there!

He is considered, sort of a justice official appointed to the official communiqué with people for delivering the imperial commandments of a God according to His whims, that were received by the agency of an intermediary institution known as **Gabriel**!.. God were to declare commands from up-there, the postman were to deliver them, and we, the door servants were to obey the commandments! The more-royalist-than-the-king servants of him-up-there, however, were to punish, beat to death and murder those who disobey the commands; and also issue court orders that "it is lawful (*vajib*) to murder such people". Marry, judge and murder all on behalf of him-up-there!

In short, **as it were, a PROPHET acting like a shadow or a loud speaker on earth for a god-up-there**!

Besides, there is the majority of people who **follows the PROPHET upon their CONJECTURE** (imaginal opinions —anxieties)!

Why should not they follow? They should of course follow, so that they may have to suffer less torment in future; even get rid of the Hellfire and enjoy Paradise forever within pleasures and felicity!

They look like those who run about after with the hope of a carrot and the fear of cudgel... At one side they try their best within both fear and hope to do what is ordered to do as much as they can; on the other side, they try to penetrate the prohibitions to enjoy the outcome of it as much as could be, assuming that they are being hidden from the eyes or from the care of Him-who-is-up-there, at all.

There is no questioning, investigation and reflection in them! Such words as "why-how-what" never cross their minds. "*Came this way,* go this way! You were for hell if you disobey, and for heaven if you obey"!!!...

Let alone the answers to the questions like "why hell?" and "what kind of heaven?", they do not even bother to take the questions into their minds! *"You know, the **Prophet** has received those commands from God up there and communicated to us as a loud speaker! Forget about the rest!"*

*"He has said, 'perform prayers (namaz)'; and you see, I bow down and stand up five times a day! Do you mean my purpose in doing them? It does not matter; what matters is that I should perform those movements and repeat the words that I do not understand! I have been obeying the orders of Him-up-there, why should not He put me into his Paradise?.. I also suffer hunger one month a year upon His request! As the Creator of universe is rewarded with my hunger, so should I be rewarded with his paradise in return!.. Why shouldn't He let me in his paradise, as I listen to His **PROPHET** and follow his imperial commands?.. Why not then?.. Besides, **I am spending so much money on sticks and stones for building schools-mosques and also for decorating His houses like palaces in the name of the RELIGION**! And why shouldn't He give me a garden house in His Paradise as a reward?.. Of course, it is none of my business if people did not know the meaning of religion at all and if they did not find answer to their questions; or if the religious understanding is in an outdated*

condition and if people cannot reach the information without payment! I cannot care about tons of people who are at the doorstep of starving to death; God should take care of them as He created them! I cannot care about millions of people, I can only build schools for a number of fifty to one hundred children and just meet their educational expenses! I am spending hundreds of billions for that!

Of course, He will put me in His Paradise in return and give me seventy beautiful houries and seventy garden houses there!.."

* * *

Such is the understanding of Muslimism that was created with so many more similar assumptions generated through the points of view that is shaped upon the understanding of **a GOD up in the sky and His public speaker-postman PROPHET**!..

Their subjection to the Prophet is one that is brought by CONJECTURE!

Dull-witted people's <u>complex of GOD-Religion-PROPHET</u> and their ways of life based on it...

* * *

Besides, there are some who follow the **RASUL of ALLAH** with their **INTELLECT** —reasoning— (*aql*)!..

Some of *Hazrat* **Mohammed's** *aleyhessalaam* companions used to call him "*Oh Nabiy<u>Allah</u>*", others "*Oh Rasul<u>Allah</u>*"!..

Never anyone called him "**Oh Prophet**!"!..

What is "*Nubuwwat*" (the quality of being *Nabi*)? What is its function? Why is one a *Nabi*? How one becomes a *Nabi*? How "*Nubuwwat*" comes into being? Where does *Nubuwwat* take its origin in a person? Why was *Hz.* **Mohammed** *aleyhessalaam* given the quality of a *Nabi*?

What is the reason behind the distinction of these two concepts from each other for such a **Person** (*Zhat*) in the **Koran** *al Karim*, instead of referring him only with the term "**Prophet**"? Why does the name "*Nabi*" is used for him in particular as a reference to the function of "*Nubuwwat*" in connection with certain definitions, while his being a "*Rasul*" and the concept of "*Risalat*" are mentioned in connection with other definitions and other functions?

What is "*Risalat*"? What is its function? For which aspect is a person a *Rasul*? How to be a *Rasul*? How does "*Risalat*" unfold in a person and where does "*Risalat*" take its root? **HOW** and for which aspects has *Hz.* **Mohammed** *aleyhessalaam* become a "**Rasul of Allah**"?

If one suggests that Rasul refers to those only who have brought a book, why then it is made clear in the chapter of Mariam (Mary), sign 54, that Ismail *aleyhessalaam* is **both a Nabi and a Rasul**, although he did not bring any book or scripture?

Without realizing these...

Without understanding what is referred to as "**ALLAH**" that *Hz.* **Mohammed** *aleyhessalaam* informed and tried to make us realize...

Without grasping the wisdom in the fact that "*WALI*" is the One who is denoted by the name **Allah**...

Without evaluating the fact that "*Sema*" (heavens) in many places of the **Koran** is cited with reference to some "**DIMENSIONS**" rather than the "**sky**"...

Without understanding that the act of "*NUZUL*" (descension) is **toward the consciousness of an individual from within his reality**, without being from the sky down to earth...

Without experiencing that "*URUJ*" (ascension) is **an ideational action of ascension toward the reality of existence from within the consciousness**...

How can one call some **PERSON** (*Zhat*) as a PROPHET and regard him as a postman or a loud speaker, while he lived all that mentioned above and consequently made the necessary announcement, showed the way toward the eternal felicity for the entire humankind as a **RASUL of ALLAH**?

Come to your senses!..

Retire in to a corner in private and start REFLECTING in a SYSTEMATIZED manner!

How can you consider the One denoted by the name "**ALLAH**", as a God sitting on the

Sirius star, considering that it is Hu that has created this universe out of a **PIN-POINT** (*nokta*), that contains billions and billions of galaxies, and that created countless **POINTS** and countless universes from each of those POINTS, and what's more, whose execution continues all the time; and how can you accept that a PROPHET is His, as it were, something between a loud speaker and a postman on earth?

If you are still for the same opinion, then I wish you happiness in your cocoon!

But if you are able to say instead, that it is impossible for you to think the same any longer...

Then, leave behind all your opinions of value and welcome the "**BOOK**" found on a shelf anew, entitled " **MOHAMMED MUSTAFA, the RASUL and the NABI of ALLAH**", that is essential to "**read**" but not read so far! (I am not speaking about a printed book made of paper for those dull-witted people!)

Start with trying to "**read**" the life stages and the **SYSTEM OF THOUGHT** of an **Intellect** who unfolded in Mecca for the purpose of becoming a "**KHALIPH**" and with a convenient *fitrat* to actualize such a purpose on a planet which is a satellite of a star among the billions of others in a galaxy beside billions of other galaxies in our universe, while all that exists only as one of the pin-points out of countless

POINTS, that what is denoted by the name "ALLAH" creates at every moment...

Try to distinct, understand how it can be for an **Intellect** to evaluate <u>the surrounding conditions, the existence as well as his own reality</u>, while taking part in this physical world bearing the *fitrat* of "**khaliphate**" beforehand and who sustained the genetic database of "*khanifism*" and found within himself the genetic heritage of a consciousness, that <u>destroyed with his hatchet (!) the recognition of angelic powers in stars as gods and also resurrected the dead bird with the power of Allah</u>?..

Such a unique consciousness (intellect)!..

Such a magnificent identity!..

Such a marvellous reformist personality!..

Did he <u>receive a PROPHETHOOD from a GOD</u> sitting in Sirius or in BETA NOVA?..

Or if not...

A "RASUL" was he and also a "NABI" of the One that is informed through the name "Allah"?

Was he a governor-commander-loud speaker delivering the imperial commandments of a god-up-in-the-sky?

Or if not...

A "**RASUL**" was he who expressed the recommendations offered with the aim of helping people realize the One denoted by the name "**Allah**" within their own reality and live its effect, through transferring them into this dimension in a manner that they all arrive from **Allah being his own reality** (*haqiqat*)?

Or a "**NABI**" of Allah was he who offered the worldly perspective and types of practices that will enable people to save themselves from endless sufferings and attain eternal felicity?

Consider it seriously now; if you live to believe in <u>God's prophet named *Hz.* Mohammed</u>**, or Mohammed Mustafa** *aleyhessalaam*, **the "Rasul" and the "Nabi" of what is denoted by the name "Allah"?**

If you believe in the latter... Then what kind of different aspects from believing in the first one do you have in your thought other than its verbosity with mere words? Pick them out and put in one side!

First of all, we must very well understand these points, so that we may start trying to "**read**" the "**BOOK**" named **MOHAMMED MUSTAFA** who is a "**RASUL**" and "**NABI**" of the One referred to as "**ALLAH**"!

Let us prepare ourselves to "read" how that Person (*zhat*) dealt with circumstances at each event, how his point of view toward events (circumstances) was, how he sought solutions in "Allah" for problems; and what it meant for him to "<u>seek solutions in Allah</u>" and how it could be; also from where to where he directed the circumstances to get a solution, why people's perspective must

be based on Allah's viewing to evaluate life and circumstances...

Besides...

We should know with certainty that...

We have not got any chance or opportunity other than being dependent on the last "**nabi**" of the One referred to as "**ALLAH**", if we want the the felicity in this world and Hereafter; and on the "**RASUL of ALLAH**" if we want to attain the One referred to as "**ALLAH**" that is our **reality**!

May Allah make us realize and comprehend this fact; facilitate its effect and bestow its digestion!

* * *

PROPHET (!?)

Do we desire to understand the **Koran** *al-Karim*?

If we want to understand and evaluate the **Koran** *al-Karim* correctly, we must at first communicate the original words of the **Koran** as they are and use those original words in every related place.

When reading the interpretations (*tafsir*) or translations (*ma'al*) of the **Koran**, please pay attention to the following point in the first place... If in a **Koran** translation, the word "**GOD**" is used instead of the word "**Allah**" in the original text and if the word "**prophet**" is employed in a translation while the words of "**Rasul**" and "**Nabi**" are cited in the original text, then please be assured that such a translation is not capable of making you reach the realities (*haqiqat*) and the mysteries (*sirr*) that are being referred in the **Koran**!

It will never be possible for you to grasp the message given to us by *Hazrat* **Mohammed Mustafa** *alayhessalam* by means of such a translation... Not even its translator has understood anything from that Book, let alone his translation to serve us!

In our various publications we have tried to discuss that the meaning of the word "**God**" has nothing to do with the meaning that is denoted by the name "**Allah**"; and that the word "**god**" associates with a religion of "**SkyGod**"...

I would like to highlight another error now, which is the usage of the word "**PROPHET**" in **Koran** translations...

We must know that every word used in the **Koran** has been specifically chosen because of their reference to particularly comprehensive and intensive meanings in their cites...

The word "**prophet**" takes its origin from the Latin word "*prophétés*" (meaning spokesman or one who speaks beforehand. Pro-, before + -phétés, "speaker". Its equivalent is "peygamber" in Turkish from **Persian** origin that Iranians speak...) It is an ancient word used in parallel to their understanding of "**god**" since the ancient times... These words are used in English and Persian to replace the meanings of both "*Rasul*" and "*Nabi*" used in the **Koran**. It is also used in the same way in our language.

"Prophet" is a word used to refer to "god's messenger".

A prophet as a messenger is used to mean a postman of a God or of a godly power in space!!!...

However...

The One denoted by the name "**Allah**" makes up the existence and origin of all the units that we can perceive or not, through Hu's names (*asma*) and attributes (*sifat*), and it is impossible to consider a limit for Hu's Essence!

In the light of this statement...

Whoever has attained "**Allah**", —not extrinsically, that is from outward—, but intrinsically, through his own existence, core, truth, realizes and understands that the existence that his name and image exhibits, is only an illusion and his being consists of "**nothing**", only the One denoted by the name "**Allah**" is all that exists...

Therefore, we need to understand that the One denoted by the name "**Allah**" is the reality of a "**naabi**", a "**rasul**" and a "**wali**", while becoming unfolded through all of Hu's esma (names) and attributes at all dimensions, and is meanwhile *Gani* (independent and free) from all those.

And they whose attributes are referred through those names [such as naabi, rasul and wali], **bring to word (verbalize) the truth of the spiritual station that they have attained dimensionally within themselves**. That is, they are not postmen (nor spokesmen) for someone afar-off, but the **tongue of what is within their own truth**!

Both "**naabi**" and "**rasul**" have attained their spiritual stations as objects of spiritual perfection of *walayat*, which is the revelation of the name "AL **WALI**" as one of the names of the One that the name "**Allah**" refers to.

Such persons carrying out their functions of *nubuwwat* and *risalat* in their worldly lives, take their perfect spiritual wisdom (*kamalat*) from the expression of the name "**WALI**" and continue their lives in the Hereafter (*akhirat*) beyond death within a spiritual state of "*risalat*" that is involved in "*walayat*"...

The One that is denoted by the name "**Allah**" has not a name known as "*Nabi*"; however, the name "*Al* **Wali**" is **Baki** (Deathless)!

"*Nubuwwat*" is a function that is valid for this world's life.

"*Risalat*" is a function valid for both this world's life and the life beyond death.

The existence of every "*nabi*", every "*rasul*" and every "*wali*" takes its origin from the truth (*haqiqa*) of "*walaya*"...

Every "*nabi*" is a "*nabi*" in consideration of his outer reality (*zakhir*) and is a "*wali*" in consideration of his inner reality (*batin*).

Every "**Rasul**" in the past is essentially a "*wali*" at the same time in view of his inner reality (*batin*) regardless of whether he was a "*nabi*" or not in view of his visible reality (*zakhir*) —from the external point of view.

Every "*wali*" takes his existence and spiritual perfection from his "*walayat*".

The execution of "*nubuwwat*" is connected with the worldly lives and it comes to an end with the transition of that "*nabi*" into the life of *akhirat*...

"*Nubuwwat*" has essentially come to an end with **Mohammed Mustafa**, who is the "*khatmun-naabi*" (the last *nabi*); there will come no other *nabi* till Doomsday.

Some of the "*anbiya*" [plural form of "*nabi*"] are at the same time "*Rasul*"... The execution of a "*rasul*" that is known as "*risalat*", is a duty valid till Doomsday.

The quality of being a "*nabi*" is temporal; "*risalat*" (being a *rasul*) is however quintessential and it does not come to an end by transition from the world, as there is no end for knowing the self and such a duty lasts eternally for *rasuls*. It is therefore that, we affirm our **witnessing** (*shahada*) for Hazrat **Mohammed's** *aleyhessalaam* being a "*Rasul*", that pertains to his eternal function, through the "words of witnessing" (*kalimatit shahadat*), meaning that we accept and confirm the **Religon of Islam**. Therefore we say "*RasuluHu*" after "*AbduHu*", never "*nabiyyuhu*"...

"*Risalat*" and "*nubuwwat*" are the highest classes in "*walayat*". Same as the class of "**general commanders**" in the commonality of "army"...

"*Nubuwwat*" is a function of informing the members of the society about the requirements of life that will make them reach <u>the bliss of Hereafter</u> (*akhirat*) and to invite people to live in accordance with those conditionals.

"*Risalat*" is to inform the members of the society <u>their own truth</u>; to communicate to them the practices and the way of life required to live its effect, and to give guidance to them on this path...

"*Ulul-azm*" is a title given to those persons who take upon the fulfillment of both the functions of "*risalat* " and "*nubuwwat*".

"*Walayat*" is to know and live (experience) one's own Truth (*haqiqat*).

In the **Koran** *al-Karim*, the word "*naabi*" has been used in wherever such functions are mentioned as those that are related to the society within the framework of "*nubuwwat*".

The word "*rasul*" has been used in wherever such functions as those that are connected with the society outwardly, are mentioned within the framework of "*risalat*".

The word "*wali*" has been used in wherever it is meant to draw the attention toward the kind of spiritual perfection that the individual should experience with regards to his life.

The positions held by the men of higher spiritual perfection based on the reality of "*walayat*" were named as *nubuwwat* and *risalat* as their functions were toward the external world; and in this manner they have been considered in a different class in comparison to the "*awliya*" [plural form of *wali*] who were experiencing (living) the inner perfection towards themselves.

If the related signs of the **Koran** are read again under the guidance of those definitions, we come across to the understandings of quite different dimensions...

On the other hand...

By another definition, those "*awliya*" who have brought a *shari'at* are called as "*naabi*", while those who have invited people to live the requirements of their own truth, without bringing a *shari'at*, are called as "*rasul*"; and those who have not taken upon such a task are called as "*wali*".

"*Walayat*" is not a sultanate inheriting from father to son but it is a result of one's experiencing the One denoted by the name "**Allah**" as being one's own truth.

When the truth, which is the basis for the perfection of "*walayat*", becomes manifest as an information in a "*naabi*" or "*rasul*" according to the rule of "*nuzul*" (descendance), it is called "*wahiy*" (divine inspiration). When the perfection of "*walayat*" becomes manifest in a "*wali*" according to the rule of "*uruj*" (ascendance), it is called as "inspiration" (*ilham*).

Employing the word "**prophet**" will not only conceal all the above mentioned facts, but will hide a lot of mysteries resulting from them from the people of understanding.

There cannot be *ibadat* with the translation of the Koran *al-Karim*!

There cannot be the translation of the Koran *al-Karim*!

The **Koran** *al-Karim* has come for the people to understand and live its requirements; therefore, everybody may give explanation within the limits of his understanding under the title 'as far as I understand from the Koran...' No matter who names it what...

The "**Gods**" may be "**great**"...

But, "**Allah**" is *akbar*!

This is the truth that our inner discovery (*kashf*) tells us... Allah knows its reality!

WasSalaam...

* * *

UNIVERSAL

One cannot understand without thinking...

The meaning that the *Deen-i* Islam is universal!

The Deen-i Islam is not a kind of information of system that came to a specific tribe or nation to speak to their particular understanding and is not aimed at guiding some of them in particular!.

Nor is the **Deen-i Islam** an understanding of religion that came specifically to speak to some nations of Arabs, Persians, Turks, Malaysians or some others!.

Deen-i Islam is a name given to the <u>universal system and order that Allah created</u>... People acquire for themselves the necessary means of attainment for peace and felicity in the dimensions of this world and beyond death, insofar as they could understand that system and mechanism.

Those who approach the Deen-i Islam with some racial (national), customary, cultural or relational (comparative) prejudice and judgements, can never realize the value

of universal realities which are meant to be informed in origin...

Within the **conceptual confusion** of our day, the **Deen-i Islam** has almost been invisible behind people's value judgements built on their parroting (*taqlid*) it afar from deep thought and questioning.

Just for the sake of conversation it is said that the **Deen-i Islam is universal**!

As this fact is denied without realizing with almost every following idea!

What is meant by a **Universal Deen**?...

It means the **Deen** that speaks to a Turk, an Arab, an American, a Mexican, an Eskimo, a Japan, Chinese, in short, **to each and every nation from an equal distance** and that aims for benefit to them all!

This is the understanding of Deen that takes source from the universal realities and that is based on the universal system. Because:

It does not come under restriction by the customs, habits and traditions of **Turks**!

It does not come under restriction by the customs, habits and traditions of **Arabs**!

It does not come under restriction by the customs, habits and traditions of **Asians** or **Eskimos**!...

As the **Rasul of Allah** *Hazrat* **Mohammed Mustafa** *aleyhessalaam* descended from the generation of *Hazrat* **Abraham** in an Arabic community, the understanding of **Deen** that he communicated has been mistakenly appropriated for Arabic communities as a great misjudgment and has then been *blended* with the customs, habits and traditions of Arabs, and so has it been tried to inject people universally in such a form!

People have been invited to a ***Muslimism that is blended with Arab people's customs, habits and traditions***, under the term that it is the **Deen-i Islam**.

This gave rise to an assumption of peoples that look from outside as that the **Deen-i Islam** were an <u>Arabic Religion</u>!

The Deen-i Islam is the explanation of the universal system and mechanism to the entire humanity by the Rasul of Allah... It is the announcement to all humankind without any racial consideration, that they who organize their lives taking these realities into account (live under the guidance of those realities) will attain the eternal peace and felicity...

Moses *aleyhessalaam* is a **Rasul and Nabii of Jewish race**, as he has came to only one race!

<u>**However, as a Rasul of Allah, universal human Mohammed** *aleyhessalaam* **has come to the entire human race, not only to one race, and he has been explaining the Universal System and Order that is created by the One that is referred to as "ALLAH".**</u>

Hazrat **Mohammed** *aleyhessalaam* is a **"UNIVERSAL RASUL"**. He invites people to see the **universal realities**! Never to see the customs, habits and the traditions of Arabs!

The customs, habits and the traditions of Arabs are their own business, regardless of whether they may be right or wrong; and they do not matter for the **universal human**!..

The customs, habits and the traditions of Turks are their own business, either right or wrong, they do not matter for the **universal human**!..

The customs, habits and the traditions of Far Easterners, Eskimos or the grandchildren of Incas are their own business, either right or wrong, they do not matter for the **universal human**!..

The Deen of the universal human is the Deen-i İslam that is universal! He does not veil, deform or degenerate **the Universal Deen Islam** with some local, attributional values or judgements; he does neither downgrade It by depreciating, not even unknowingly!

All people are unavoidably dependent on (under the authority of) the system and mechanism informed by the Deen and besides, they will have to pay for the cost of neglecting its requirements as to the degree of their negligence!

The Muslimism, that is advertised as the true religion in market after it is blended

with some national customs, habits and traditions of nations, differs from the **universal Deen-i Islam** in quite many aspects and it therefore fails to receive a universal acceptance and is rejected!

If this **_Muslimism_** that is blended with some national (racial) features and though imposed after being labeled as the "**underline**universal** religion of Islam**" has not received and is not receiving widespread approval by the majority of the world's people on this day, it is because of the presentation of the **Deen-i Islam** in the form of a _National Religion_!.. People are invited to the **Arab Muslimism under the term of** "**Deen-i Islam**". As a result of this, they have been fighting against each other all the time! This is a very big malfeasance!

It is extremely difficult for the people that have not reached the universality, to estimate and appreciate the universal **Rasul of Allah**!.. So is for them to understand the **Universal Deen**, as a consequence.

Though the universal humans who could grasp this, show respect to all the customs, habits and traditions, they never depend on such **local and RELATIVE (ATTIBUTIONAL) values**; same as Jalaluddini Rumi, Shamsi Tabrizi, Yunus Emre, Hadji Baktash Wali did!..

Rasul of Allah, the universal human Mohammed Mustafa _aleyhessalaam_... The universal _awliyah_ (friends) of Allah... Universal humans... Universal Book... The Speech that is full of Universal Mysteries... And its **"READers"**...

The religions of races or nations... Prophets of nations!.. Imitator (*muqallid*) members of religions... National *awliyah* along with those *qutb*, *ghauws* and *mahdis* of every district... Distorted translations of the Koran...

Along with some **religious understandings** based on Totems or a **"Sky-God"**, that are born out of the consideration of a God, the prophet of that God and the translations of the Koran prescribing a God as a He-God!

Besides is the exhibition of all those in a basket with a label that it is the **Religion of Islam**.

In order to be able to "**READ**" the **Deen-i Islam** that explains the universal realities as informed by the **universal Rasul of Allah Mohammed Mustafa** *aleyhessalaam*, and the **universal Book** the **Koran** *al Karim*, first of all, it is necessary for us to understand, learn and digest in moderation *what the universality is and how it is to be*; and then, to consider that Book with such a viewing!..

It is necessary to comprehend and digest in moderation that the *sunnat* of RasulAllah Mohammed Mustafa *aleyhessalaam* is not Arabian customs and habits but the *Sunnat of Allah*, along with the meaning of what the "*Sunnat* of Allah" is!.

It is necessary to "READ" (*iqraa*) the Rasul of Allah Mohammed Mustafa *aleyhessalaam*!.

So that from then onward one could perceive what the **Universal Deen-i Islam** is... And only after than that this reality that is perceived, can be confirmed or rejected!

"*Alhamdulillah, I am a Muslim!*"

"*Inshaallah* you are a Muslim!!???."

If these are mere words uttered on parroting, the state of one who utters them is like a person who says he knows swimming but in actuality he has never seen a sea in his life and who thus informs his own reality!.

It is a very important question to answer what benefit can come through putting and repeating some certain words into a person's brain which is conditioned and blocked with some local and RELATIVE judgements and who has not heard of what universality is.

It is impossible for a person who is not aware of what it is to be "**universal**", to realize the value of the **Universal Deen, the Universal Rasul and the universal human**!.

Actually, the universal Rasul of Allah, universal Mohammed Mustafa *aleyhessalaam* invites people to confirm Islam as the universal Deen and to live its effect!.

Therefore, we need urgently to refine ourselves from our national understanding of religion in order to realize and grasp the universal **Deen-i Islam** and we should try to "READ" (*iqraa*) **Rasul of Allah Mohammed Mustafa** *aleyhessalaam* **with respect to his universality** rather than his Arabic hereditary, so that we may begin to realize some certain facts.

* * *

Chapter 6

The KORAN

Verily we have put forth for men, in this
Koran every kind of Parable. in order that
they may receive admonition.
(The Koran: 39/27)

And verily We have displayed our warnings
in this Koran that they may take heed.
(17/41)

And verily We have displayed for mankind in
this Koran all manner of similitudes, but man
is more than anything contentious.
(18/54)

THE SOUL OF THE KORAN

As an outcome of their failure to **READ** the **SOUL** of our holy book **Koran** *al-Karim*, I often come across with the following criticizing question of some people who are against the **Religion of Islam** informed by **Mohammed** *aleyhessalaam* as a "**Rasul of Allah**"...

Here is their criticizing question:

"*Hazrat* Mohammed has come some 14 hundred years ago as a prophet to a society of about five thousand people, the majority of which consisted of people with primitive level of understanding. According to their understanding, the little daughters were buried alive and killed in the sand thinking that they would make their fathers ashamed when they grow up. Women could be sold and bought like a commodity for countless times as they were not considered as humans and they had no rights. Of course in such a society the questions and the problems had taken form according to the prevailing level of understanding of people of those days and the solution for those questions and problems were the means for the formation of the Koran.

If *Hazrat* Mohammed had come to the world in the Poles instead of his area of birth, the book he was going to communicate at his time of prophethood, would take form according to the questions and problems regarding the social conditions, customs and traditions of Eskimos.

In this case, as no other prophet nor a book will come as informed by that Book itself, then how can the people of our age, be controlled with those rules set up for such a community with an obvious level of understanding?.. Wouldn't those rules make this book invalid even for yesterday or today, let alone reach beyond the coming centuries. How can it be possible to speak to the countless societies living all over the world today with the rules that have been formed according to the prevailing understanding of some 14 hundred years ago? Is the Koran going to let people into heaven by taking them back to 1400 years?

Yes, this is the question that latest atheists put forward within their perspective based on their level of understanding!.

It may be true or false, but, **in my humble opinion**, here is the answer to them…

Considering those who understand the **"SOUL"** of the Koran *al-Karim*, it is a **Book** that involves the information to enlighten people and to provide them with the bliss of Hereafter (*akhirat*), as long as humanity exists!..

Moreover, in most parts it opens people the information and life requirements that will be benefited forever including even the dimensions of hell and heaven... It explains the **truth of human** and what the name "**ALLAH**" refers to!

In my previous discussions, I have made it clear that the information in the **Koran** in some parts originates from the perfect spiritual wisdom (*kamalat*) of "*nubuwwa*" while the other parts from the perfect spiritual wisdom of "*risalat*"; and that information originated from the perfection of *risalat* will eternally rule (be on the agenda) and will be able to make people gain new unfoldments (developments)... They are like the Chapters of "*ikhlas*" and "*Fatiha*" communicated through the spiritual perfection of "*Risalat*".

Such themes as marriage, inheritance, right of testimony and retaliation that originate from the perfect spiritual wisdom of *Nubuwwa* and that guide people's social life within a community, are statements (*hukm*) that carry weight as long as a person lives in this world and they disappear with person's death.

Let us now try to perceive and understand the **SOUL of the Koran** *al-Karim*....

Is the Koran a book which has been communicated to us with an aim of taking people backwards, towards the primitive life of centuries ago, to fix and lock them into that reverted way of life?.. Or else... Does it guide people to get prepared for future and

show them the ways to advancement - perfection and turn them towards what is the most perfect?..

Hazrat **Ali** whom I believe to be one of the leading figures among those who have understood that great book best, has said the following as a result of that understanding:

"Bring up your children not for the time that you live, but for the time that they will live!."

Such a (futuristic) life style and the **point of view ahead of its time** belongs to a Person who has spent with *Hazrat* **Mohammed** *aleyhessalaam* all his boyhood and young years and who has obtained the **SOUL of the Koran from Him**...

Considering the statements that nourish societies through the spring of *nubuwwa*... All of them are aimed to verify the **rights of womanhood** for females merely, who has been ignored as humans and treated as **commercial sex materials** until then since the early times. Treating them as commercial goods has been disallowed (forbidden), they were provided with certain rights as a **spouse** and their right of "**testifying**" as witnesses has been admitted while they had no voice in society at that time and also their rights to **take share from the inheritance** have been established!..

Now, please, try now to grasp the following fact with understanding and insight:

Regarding its **SOUL**, the **Koran** has brought commands (statements) aimed to prevent from getting stuck with the past, to stop going backwards, to eliminate injustice (unfairness) and to encourage people always consider matters with respect to the future conditions!..

BESIDES… Believing that it may help to **understand the Koran more realistically**, I should point out the following as my personal opinion, that does not oblige anybody…

While bringing those commands, the Koran does not say that you should not establish an equality by means of increasing those rights and you should not move forward but should remain where you are without advancement and let woman remain as a second class!.

While confining the right of **possessing numerous females** down to four as a progress, it warns that it is much more beneficial to live **with a single wife** and this is set as a **goal**…

While *Zakat* is informed as a minimum right for people, it is besides considered excellent to share what is in your possession as much as possible in terms of charity.

I mean, these **rights acknowledged for woman** are not their ultimate rights and are not limited there, but they are the basics for the system of rights that should be developed in proportion with the evolution of the society, the men and the women…

If the woman who had no right of voice has been given the right to be a witness together with another woman, it does not mean that this condition will remain the same forever. In my opinion, it means that the woman may have equal rights with men proportional to their advancement! At least it has been made possible for "**women who had no right of voice**," to live as a human and to "**give their testimony**" together with another woman. That means, in time, when you, as the members of the society come to appreciate the value of women; when you start noticing that <u>**she too is a servant of Allah like yourselves, that she has a place on earth as a human and a "KHALIPH"**</u>, you should not hinder her from having equal rights with man.

<u>If a society recognizes the right of testifying for one woman together with a man, it will never contradict with the "**SOUL**" of the Koran in my understanding; and furthermore, this is more appropriate…</u>

While **a woman, who had no share in a heritage**, is provided with the right of having at least half as much as that of a man according to the conditions in those days, it does not mean that, **mind you, any more of it should be avoided**!.. On the contrary, it is a sign of a society's advancement in accordance with the "**SOUL**" of the Koran to give equal shares…

<u>**In other words, the SOUL of the Koran has determined the bottom limits with those**</u>

commands to prevent going backwards, but it has never put a limit for progressive practices, according to my understanding...

It is therefore that there is no need for another book to come after the Koran, and in this respect, *Hazrat* Mohammed *aleyhessalaam* has been the last of all the prophets (*khatamun nabii*), as it explains human rights without bringing any limitation for progress and because it has that futuristic (open for advancement) understanding.

The **Koran** that reveals the system **in terms of afterlife conditions and of knowing Allah, through** [the medium of] *risalat*, has improved, developed human rights as much as possible within the existing conditions of that day, and determined them as the bottom limits without bringing any forbiddance to further advancement in due course of time, through [the medium of] "*nubuwwa*".

That **basic principle** is the "**SOUL of the Koran**" as far as I understand, which provides that *Aziz* (Magnificent) Book with eternal validity without any necessity for another book to come.

* * *

TO "READ" THE KORAN

We felt that we had to return to the same topic that we have discussed in our previous article entitled "**The SOUL of The Koran**" and give further explanations, as it was misunderstood by some dull-witted people.

In our day, being able to read the words in Arabic letters (even without knowing their meaning) is assumed to be "**reading the Koran**"... Some people however, consider reading Koran translations (*ma'al*) as "**reading the Koran**"... These are only the preliminary stages of "**reading**" the **Koran**...

Yet, in my opinion, such forms of readings cannot be regarded as **"READING" the Koran**!

As we have referred to "**READING**" the **System**...

We can also refer to **"READING" the Koran**...

How is it possible to really **READ the Koran**?

READING the Koran is only possible through perceiving "**the SOUL of the Koran**"!

What does it mean to perceive the "**the SOUL of the Koran**"?

What is the purpose that the **Koran** *al-Karim* has been revealed for mankind?

What kinds of benefits does the **Koran** *al-Karim* provide people with that it has been revealed to?

What kind of a life does the **Koran** *al-Karim* prepare mankind for, that it has been revealed to?

What kind of qualities of human does The **Koran** *al-Karim* inform people that it has been revealed to?

Has the Koran *al-Karim* been revealed with an aim to limit, fix and lock people into a form of life, and seal the doors to advancement or, is it aimed at showing them the ways of advancing steadfastly, to provide them with rights that they are not aware of or that have been taken away, and to inform them of the ways to live with the faculties of being a "khaliph" man and woman alike, as a consequence?

Do the signs in the **Koran** *al-Karim* that were revealed, involve an aim that man should live showing respect for the rights of fellow human beings yet live a progressive life permanently, or have they been revealed aiming towards a regressive life for mankind?

If we can answer these questions correctly, we will have placed the first stepping stone towards understanding "the **SOUL of the Koran**" whereby, the rest of the stones will fall into place until a staircase is built which leads us to open the door of "**READING**" the **Koran al-Karim.**

As a result of our **misunderstanding**, the Koran has been locked in chains and turned into a holy book from ancient times, which rests on dusty shelves!

Yet, <u>**with regards to its "SOUL" and its "OBJECTIVES", the Koran upholds such properties as to enlighten and guide mankind as long as humanity exists**</u>, that it is therefore a Book <u>ABOVE ALL TIMES</u>!

Restraining the **Koran** *al-Karim* with the progressions and reforms it brought to the societies it came, by saying "<u>its service for humanity has finished at that point and is outdated, therefore it is a book belonging to that period only of those ancient times</u>", is an **injustice** (*zulm*) **to the Koran**. This results from the inability to perceive the "**SOUL of the Koran**" and to READ the Koran!

While the **Koran** suggests giving <u>one fortieth</u> of your possessions within the framework of *Zakat* (alms), it does not in any way bring any restrictions about giving one twentieth of it! The former is to be understood as the minimum and not so much as to be the "be all and end all" of alms per se...

While having no inheritance rights at all, as a minimum amount women were allowed, by the

Koran, half of the share given to a man... However, if you decided to give a share equal to that of a man, it would never contradict with the "**SOUL of the Koran**". Besides, the **Koran does not restrict this, but instead it welcomes progression in accordance with its SOUL**!

I mean that, the **rights and reforms brought by the Koran** need to be considered as the minimum that cannot be taken backwards. **There is neither a sign in the Koran nor an indication from RasulAllah that progress cannot be made towards the maximum of rights!**

As a result of the failure in understanding the "SOUL of the Koran", the Koran is not READ and thus, people hold onto its surface verbalism, literal meaning. The unfortunate consequence is that the given message is lost!

What's more, upon RESTRAINING the **Koran al-Karim** with a dull-witted understanding, it is wrongfully concluded that "the Koran can not be applied to our days"!

When need arises to create a law, the main factor in its establishment is **in fact the soul of such a law**, which demands that law to be established. An adequate fashion of rendering (statement) is determined in connection with that soul, that is the prospect of thought, and it is verbalized and therewith an article of law is brought into existence... When a judge needs to exercise this law, he establishes a connection between the given event and his own perspective of judicious reasoning about that event and makes a judgment **based on the main reason that has formed the law**.

If a judge sets his opinion about an event by taking the law within the surface verbalism rather than respecting the soul of that law, he is most likely to misjudge! A judicial decision must be **based not on the literal aspect of a law but on its soul**!

Laws exist along with their souls. If they are taken in mere verbalism, DEVIATIONS from the goal will take place! The conscience of a judge is there to help the judicious reasoning of an event be based on the soul of law!

In the same way, to be able to **"READ" the Koran**, it is necessary to consider the purpose for which the verses regarding a particular event were revealed, and the benefits that these verses aim to provide man and women with. All the evaluations must be based on these facts.

The **Koran al-Karim** has made the greatest revolutions in the history of mankind. Due to the inability in perceiving this SPIRIT of the **Koran al-Karim**, looking at only the words of the **Koran** on the surface and commenting that "*that's all it has given to humankind, it does not give anything beyond these, but bring restrictions,*" is the greatest of blindness and darkness (oppression).

It cannot be described other than as an **ulterior motive to deviate the reality** by imposing such a perspective as if "Islam affirms slavery" while in fact it regards deliverance of a slave as one of the greatest *ibadat* (practices) and so aims at ending slavery in a society where it was common.

It is an enormous injustice done to the ***Deen-i Islam*** and is a plain result of not understanding the **"SOUL" of the Koran** to disapprove it by assuming it as an assertive and coercive religious understanding, whereas **Islam does not condone using force in any point** except putting an end to violations on human rights, and despite the known sign to the Rasul that "**you are not one to force them**"!

Democracy can only be found within the principals of ***Deen-i* Islam** in the most comprehensive sense; because the **Koran *al-Karim*** does not **allow pressure to be put on people** in any regard.

The Koran *al-Karim* ADVISES mankind on **essential ideas** they need so that their future may bring them peace and blessings. It informs mankind of what is to come hereafter and what they need to do, and notes that those who practice them will find reward, and warns those who do not, about the regrets that they will fall into in the afterlife because of the conditions that will be encountered, and that they will never be able to turn back from there nor made up for the past... **After this point, neither a**

person nor a government has an authority to FORCE anybody to practice them, with respect to the "SOUL" of _Deen-i_ Islam... As a matter of fact, every person will appraise and attach importance to those proposals with their own mind and reasoning, and will practice as they wish without anyone's pressure, and will finally reach their result!

The unknowing and ignorant persons' false convictions, which is acquired due to their inability to read the **"SOUL" of the Koran _al-Karim_**, can never be connected with the **_Deen_** of **Islam**!

There cannot be an excuse made for staying away from Islam and the Koran, because of being overwhelmed with false interpretations of those who cannot "**READ**" the **Koran _al-Karim_**!

Every INDIVIDUAL is responsible of READING the Koran and learning _Deen-i_ Islam personally, for their own future. To make excuses for the mistakes that it was the practice of other Muslims in my surroundings, is of no importance. Learning the _Deen_ **by following the Koran, rather than by following the Muslims** is essential (_fard_) for everybody. Those who fail to do so will suffer its consequences in the Hereafter (_akhirat_).

Therefore, we must now realize that...

It is the most rewarding (helpful) practice for a person **to READ, appreciate and make use of the Koran _al-Karim_**, that has been revealed to make the women and men, namely all the believers, become aware of the fact that they have been created as a "khaliph" and experience its effect; through letting them know the conditions of life beyond death and teaching them the ways of having a wonderful life of beauties beyond death. One who practices it will have its benefits, and one who disregards it, will suffer the result of his negligence in the Hereafter.

Neither the One who is denoted by the name "**ALLAH**", nor **Rasulullah Muhammed Mustafa** *aleyhessalaam* is in need of our beliefs and our practices as te requirements of our beliefs, because all proposals have been made to the PERSON individually and concern their own future...

Happy are those who can **"READ" the Koran and live its effect**...

* * *

Chapter 7

The **FAITH**

The desert Arabs say:
"We have faith"…
Say: "You have no faith!…
But you only perform actions of the faithful."
Not yet has Faith entered into their consciousness
(heartfelt consideration).
But if they obey ALLAH and Hu's Rasul, their
deeds will not be diminished aught of!…
*The **Koran** (Hujuraat: 14-15)*

HOW TO GET OUT OF HELL

During my three-month visit to London in the summer of 1996, I gave many talks about these matters on London Turkish Radio live for two hours a day. Meanwhile, I have also tried to give answers to questions from listeners, as far as I know.

Two of the questions were rather interesting. The first question was this:

"Why will most people stay in Hell for ever and will not get out of it to enter for Heaven?"

The second was as follows:

"You all Muslims keep talking about the existence of Allah! Is there anyone in history, who has seen Allah, so that we could believe in?"

Let us first mention the following facts:

After the great crowd known as Judgement Day, the entire human race without exception will find themselves in the environment called as Hell. In the following stages, people of **faith** (*iman*) will move past through it and reach to the environment of Heaven. **People of denial** (who lack *iman*), however, will abide in the environment of Hell forever. It means that the ability to pass through Hell and reach to Heaven is not a result of a person's practice or deed, but it is totally related with a matter of "**faith**" (*iman*).

The duration of someone's stay in Hell and his spiritual level in Heaven, however, are totally depended on his actions and practices he achieved in the world.

Why should it be depended on one's "faith" to access Heaven? I will try to explain it!

Some cases of paralysis simply stem from psychological reasons. Despite the lack of any pathological symptoms determined physically, a person, who may have **conjectured** himself paralyzed and unable to walk again, can spend a life of Hell on a wheeled chair. Some people, who may be said "addictive of sickness," **cannot utilize their mind properly due to their faculty of "conjecture" (*wahm*) overpowering themselves**, and cannot execute their capabilities and as such they cannot get out of the Hell that turn their life into an affliction.

As we have discussed widely in our book "**REASONING AND BELIEF,**" no one can overwhelm the influence of conjecture (distrust) that turns one's life into hell, through the help of reasoning. The power within human to overwhelm the **force of conjecture**, which means "**assuming there is what there is not and there is not what there is,**" is not his faculty of reasoning but is rather his faculty of "believing." While conjecture easily rules over reasoning and the mechanism of thought, it is always defeated by the power of belief (*iman*), which exercises direct influence on actions. It is therefore that the people of reasoning have been proposed to understand the *Deen* with mind and to take further steps with faith.

Man's hell in his worldly life as well as in the next, is just a result of the **power of his conjecture overwhelming** him. It is only by means of his **command of belief** (*iman*) that conjecture can be expelled.

If a person assuming himself paralyzed despite the unavailability of any physical defect, can meet with someone whom he can have faith in, he will walk! A suspicious person's suffering will come to an end when he encounters a person or an information to have faith on.

In the most trivial sense, **believing in Allah results in a person's belief that he will receive help from the attributes that belong to Allah, whenever he comes across with a difficulty, and thus he will be rescued from there into peace (*salamat*).** A person holding such a belief will find the power within to rescue himself from the Hell environment, even if his belief was as little as an atom's weight. But, if a person does not hold such a belief and assumes himself restricted with normal physical powers and **if he does not understand and neither believe in Allah,** he will never be able to get out of Hell as **he will suffer the lack of the potential powers that belongs to Allah within himself.** Since he does not believe in for himself, no one else will be able to help him there, no matter who the other was; same as a person who assumed himself unable to walk because of his skepticism overpowering his mind.

It means that, the reason of imprisonment in Hell for those who will permanently abide in Hell, is **their spending their lifetimes without belief because of their failure in freeing themselves from the power of their conjecture that commands their lives.**

Let us come to the answer for the second question.

That listener constructed his logic such as the following:

If something cannot be seen with eye, it simply does not exist.

Considering that the object called as "Allah" is not seen with eye, then it does not exist. As we have never seen Allah even after we opened up the solid matter, there is not Allah and we cannot accept such an existence.

It was not possible to give a detailed answer to this question on air, so I briefly gave an answer with the following question:

"**Saying that you cannot see Allah in the physical world, you reach a conclusion that there is not Allah! If the same logical construct that you use is carried on... We are not able to see what is** "mind" **in a brain even after we open it by surgery. Once we cannot see your mind, should we then result that you are** "mindless?""

The line went off!

The basic mistake of that listener is as follows:

"In his world of thought that he constructed on various misinformation, he used to assume the existence of a separate god-out-there and he labeled such a god as "**Allah**," as the noun employed by Muslims. Alike many people calling themselves **Muslims**, he also was unaware of the being denoted by the name "Allah" as explained in the **Koran *al Karim.***

Stated briefly, **calling the imagined god he constructed in his mind by the name** "Allah" and then arriving at a judgement that there cannot be such an irrationality, he claims the nonexistence of that god. I mean it was his assumed (imagined) god that he denied and not what he had no information about...

I regret to tell that all those who are not Muslims as well as those who consider themselves Muslims and **criticize what is denoted by the name** "Allah," do just talk about their imagination of deity they make up in their minds.

What the name "**Allah**" denotes is, however, free from such primitive description...

* * *

KNOWING "FAITH" IS NOT "FAITH"

The issue of religion covers rather a large area in our lives...

Most of us are watchful over our Religion and do not allow anyone to speak ill of it, even though we may never be [concerned about] practicing it...

It all sounds fine, but can one be a Muslim by saying "**I am Muslim**"?..

Can one be a *mu'min* (man of faith) by saying "**I am a believer**"?...

Let us first focus on the following point: What does the sentence "**I am a *mu'min***" mean?.. Why do we use this statement?.. What do we need to know while we are pronouncing it and what do we need to understand when it is pronounced?

We should know before all that to **have "faith" (*iman*) is a constitutional (*fitri*) [natural — inborn] characteristic**. It can never be acquired after birth!. It can be unfolded from within some time afterwards but it can never be obtained thereafter!.

What does it mean, "the unfoldment of *iman* (faith) from within a person"?

"*Iman*" (faith) refers to a person's [capability of] perception through insight (*basirat*) that beyond his individualized consciousness (the already known personality) that one assumes for himself, there is only **ONE Single Authority** that is constituting (making up) everything according to Its own will…

"<u>*Iman*</u>" **(faith) enables one to access the dimension known as "heaven" by getting freed from the dimension of hell. "<u>Islam</u>" however, enables one to escape from the burning from the dimension of "hell" as fast as possible and provides one with a superior level of living in the dimension of heaven once it is accessible!..**

"**Having faith (*iman*) in what the *anbiya* (prophets) of Allah have announced**" is considered within this context of *iman* as mentioned here, as One Single Being's informing Its own system through the speech of the dimension known as *Nubuwwat* (prophethood)…

Being unaware of a prophet even, an ancient tribal native in the midst of Africa, can reach the dimension of heaven once this "*iman*" (belief) that we have mentioned first, is unfolded in himself…

On the other hand, so many people who do not lift up their heads from prostration (*sajda*) in a Muslim environment all long their lifetimes, might have been <u>pretending to have faith</u> and living with an "**imitated faith**" (*iman taqlid*) due to the lack of the above mentioned constitutional —inborn— *iman* in them and they might pass into the afterlife dimension as **faithless**.

Let us dwell some more on the first category of *iman*...

The **faithful** will not suffer burning while passing through hell!.. It should be known for certain that the **sufference of fiery** (burning) is because of **faithlessness**!.. <u>**Afire** is such a "**state**" that you wish to desist from and in that you feel worried, troubled, stressed and full of hatred for your life!..</u>

The insight which realizes that everything has come into being upon the ordainment (taqdir), will and creating of the One and that there was no other possibility (alternative) for what has already happened other than the way it has taken place; can live and perceive this with the **light** (nuur) **of iman** that has unfolded from within an **insight** (basirat). Upon having such an **iman**, a person will **ultimately** become an inhabitant of the dimension heaven, although he may not have seen or heard of a Nabi of Allah.

It does not matter if the words "**I am *mu'min* —a believer**" are pronounced through lips, for its outcome can only be experienced if it comes to life through one's spiritual **state** (*hal*).

There is no gain in speaking the words "**I am a Muslim**" through lips, so long as the **actions** (*fiil*) do not speak of it.

As we have already discussed in our different publications, the word "**ALLAH**" is just a name and it is necessary to focus on the understanding that this name denotes...

The manifestation of a consideration about "**what** and **how to believe in**" through ourselves, is what matters. Hence, we need to focus on how we should understand the meaning of the word "***iman***"...

"***Iman***" can first be understood in the context involving entire humankind...

"***Iman***" can secondly be understood in the context considering the believers in a *Nabi* of Allah...

In the context considering the entire humankind and involving a rough understanding of the system, "***iman***" may unfold in a person as a ***fitri* (constitutional) characteristic** and it may serve him advance to experience the dimension of heaven at the end after long periods of refinement, even if he did not recognize a *nabi*!

As for the "***iman***" in the context regarding those people who have recognized the *nabi*...

In actuality, believing in a *nabi* is a subdivision of "imitative faith" (*iman-i taqlid*)!..

Because, believing in the announcements of a *nabi* is still a "pretended" faith (*iman taqlid*) as long as it is not a belief in what is denoted by the name "ALLAH", with reference to the understanding that the mystery of "*B*" covers.[*]

It is only possible by comprehending and experiencing the mystery of "*B*" that a "pretended *iman*" may be transformed into an *iqaan* (certainty) through *tahqiq* (verification).

The point that we need to focus on here, is the fact that, to have information on *iman* is not enough and installing files of information about *iman* onto a computer to fill up its free space, will not make it experience and live the dimension of heaven.

You may setup a PC with an unimaginable amount of detailed information about "*iman*" and that PC may be configured to perform them all audio and visual at any given moment... But it does not mean it is a person of faith!..

Let us now return to the question why we needed "*iman*" and answer it briefly...

As we have mentioned above, "*iman*" **is the recognition of the fact that we have been living within the circumstances created by One single *Fatir* (Builder) in the way It wills...**

---

[*] The initial B at the beginning of "besmele: "**B**-ismi-llah-ir'Rahman-ir'Rahim" or in the "Amantu **B**i'Llahi".

If so... **Then the person can no longer observe anything labeled as "improper" or "wrong" or "inappropriate that should not have taken place" in life. Because there is only the Single One who creates all things according to Its will and who observes (journeys) whatever It has created in the way It wills!..**

Such an understanding concludes at a person's state of being well-pleased (*radhi*) with all things, such that the "**pain of burning**" in the dimension of "**hell**" ceases to exist for him. Then, the fire of hell begins to speak to him saying: "O believer! Pass over my fire quickly as your light of *iman* is blowing out my flames"!.. As known, it is only the light of *iman* that puts out the hell fire!..

Now we need to focus especially on the following:

It is not the information about *iman* that puts off the "fire" but the application (practice) of *iman*, that is to live upon *iman*.

What is meant by the application of *iman*, is a person's thinking within the scope of the "*iman* fact" that he perceives, and his realizing the value of life and the events under the illumination of his "light of *iman*"...

A person may either give consideration to (appreciate) life and events under the illumination of the light of *iman* and attains the spiritual state known as "*Radhiyya*" and experience its outcome as a man of faith, if nothing else... Or he continues suffering the pain of burning resulted from his inefficiency in "*iman*" (having faith) till he [gets used to this and] finally becomes fire-proof, so to say...

To sum up, **the information about *iman* is not *iman* itself**!

Because, "*iman*" yields a life in which: a) It enables a person to live heavenly dimensions by getting freed from burning; b) It becomes a means for an upper-dimension of heaven beyond description to come into view, through the experience of what is denoted by the name Allah in every point of being!

The <u>knowledge</u> of *iman*, on the other hand, is like a load of books on the back of a donkey... A person may carry the knowledge of *iman* in his brain (mind) and lips all along his lifetime, but he goes on burning in circumstances... He burns by throwing such accusations as "why that happens this way?", "I wish it wouldn't have happened!" and the other flames of sentimentalism brought along those accusations!.

The purpose of giving the knowledge of "*iman*" to a person is not to make him carry it but rather to experience its understanding!.

If you are living to carry the "knowledge of *iman*", your pain of burning will last as long as you are alive; your dimension will be altered as you keep on burning and your life

will last in fire eternally... It will be the same till *iman* is manifested from within you!..

If you have "*iman*", <u>its proof</u> is the fact that "burning" has ended up for you and you "<u>never throw accusations</u>" and you never find anything improper in any point in life no matter what... You may then constantly live the outcome of such an awareness and continue your "journey" (reflection) in the dimension of heaven...

Furthermore, if the mystery of "*B*" is disclosed and if you attain a spiritual state in which you live the consequences of such an unfoldment, it is only the following, that may fall from your lips:

"It is none other than Hu who contemplates"!..

* * *

WHY TO BELIEVE?

What does it mean "**for Allah**", that is "*fiiSabiilAllah*"?

<u>**It is a way of life with the experience of what is in your essence and with the fulfillment of its effect!..**</u>

That is to live with the character traits of Allah, evaluate all the beings, the entire creation with the viewing of Allah, regardless of whether they are close to or far away from you.

<u>**It means striving with your entire being to help others attain Allah, so that the *ridha* (total acceptance) of Allah may unfold through them!**</u>

<u>**What is known as "coming together for Allah" is a "togetherness" sharing that goal!**</u>

A person's unawareness of <u>**"Allah" at his core**</u> and of the experience of its effect, is what is known as "**being afflicted with the wrath (*ghazab*)**"!...

Ignoring our current state of "**affliction**" by misinterpreting the **wrath (*ghazab*)** as a fire or a suffering to come in future, is a plain state of "**affliction with Allah's wrath**"!.

"**A person who <u>has undergone the wrath of Allah</u>**", **is the one who could not recognize Allah in his very core and who still fails to experience its effect!.**

Failure in perceiving this fact is also a sign of affliction with the wrath!.."

* * *

We have given considerable emphasis to this matter in our previous chapter.

Since it is the most important subject in a human's life, I would like to carry on with explaining the same matter this time also as far as it is unfolded through ourselves.

Iman (faith) is either **manifested in a person** and he lives upon the **perspective resulting from his faith** as much as his share (*nasib*) allows him, hence he is known as a "*said*" (blessed person) as his final destination in his eternal life will be in **heaven**!..

Or else, he **lacks *iman*** at his *fitra* (innate disposition, primordial nature) and **lives upon the perspective resulting from its lack, behaves and acts within the frameworkof that perspective**, hence he is known as "*shaqi*" **(wretched)** as his final destination in his eternal life will be the dimension of "**hell**" and his life will continue in "**afire**"!

The faith "*iman*" in the person's *fitrat* will sooner or later make him realize that **Allah is**

the creator of all affairs and actions and **Allah is the executor in (having use and disposal** *–tasarruf–* **of) every single particle of the entire creation according to Hu's own will**, and as a result, faith brings that person's burning on account of that particular event to an end! Let us now recall the sign: **"Hearts will find ease with the remembrance of Allah"**...

Presence and absence of *iman* **(faith) in a** person, is the result of an unfoldment of a certain circuit of perception in his brain. I can even personally admit that there is a **gene of "***iman***"**, in my opinion!... **A brain's conclusions through interpreting circumstances under the light (***nuur***) of** *iman*, **is different from the conclusions of a brain that interprets circumstances without the light of** *iman*!.

We can never know from outside if people are carrying that gene or not!. However, their conduct of behavior may be a partial indicator for that given moment...

After all, even if we may say "this is because of the light (*nuur*) of iman" or "this is the outcome of his faithlessness" by merely looking at someone's actions, we can never make definite judgements such as a "**believer**" or an "**unbeliever**", because we cannot know in a later phase the **state of consciousness he will be having during his transition into spiritual dimension**.

In general, understanding life from a perspective based on faithlessness however, does not make a promise a happy future as a rule!.

No one's state can be truly estimated before his lifetime ends, even if he has lived upon a perspective based on *iman*.

As far as I could recall it, one of the warnings of RasulAllah *aleyhessalaam* is briefly as follows:

"A person who is known to have been murdered while fighting on the path of Allah, is said to have died while fighting to show his power and skills so that he could find favor and esteem in people's eyes and therefore he is not a *shehid* (martyr) but he is destined to hell...

A person who gives away large sums of *zakat* and alms is also said to have given away his goods to find glory in people's eyes and to bribe their hearts as he could not treat them the other way; and his deeds are not welcomed; and therefore, he is thrown into hell by angels...

An *alim* (master) is said to have communicated his knowledge to provide sustanence for himself by expecting people's favor, service and recognition as a wise person, and therefore his deeds are not rewarded and his place is hell..."

Considering this point of view, we realize that...

A believer will get the reward of his achievements provided that he has carried through all his deeds "**for Allah**" (*fii SabilAllah*), that is, for the purpose of sharing all that he had in hand, with others in his surroundings without expecting any gain in return!

All other purposes apart from this are results of a faithless point of view, that is known as "**associating partners**" (*shirk*)!

* * *

Let us examine our intentions and our points of view toward life and our surroundings, if "**wrath**" has not enveloped us, and if our conscience can see our intentions with insight, even through a needle's hole!..

Let us account for ourselves right now without waiting for tomorrow!..

Let us look at a mirror!.

Let us consider the following warning fairly: "**You are responsible for what is in your mind**"... (Bakara:284)

To be honest and open for Allah?

˙ Or to cover the faults for the sake of your material or spiritual interests and keeping your comfort safe by stating the excuse that you are doing so in order not to offend the others?

Never forget the fact that tomorrow we will lose all that is in our hands at present, no matter what!

Is it worth turning our eternal lives into hell for worthless temporary advantages?

What is more, if we are not speaking out the facts that we know, for keeping the privilege of our present advantages and if we are closing our eyes to people's following the wrong paths!..

Are we really so strong to suffer for their <u>sins</u>?..

Besides, if we do not share our knowledge with those whom we claim to be dear to us and close our eyes to the development of their gangrened condition, for the favor of our worldly comfort and self-interests, how are we going to face the account of such an oppression?

<u>*İman* will finally bring the experience of a life "*fiiSabilAllah*", as an outcome.. It makes one challenge to lose all his worldly riches!... It makes one do his best to prevent his truly-loved-companions from the fiery of tomorrow!..</u>

Iman urges one to strive with his wealth, life and wisdom to fulfill what is necessary to prevent his beloved fellowmen from falling into a house on fire.

If a person lacks the light (*nuur*) of *iman*, he only considers spending every day in more comfort! He is not concerned about afterlife conditions or of what people are going to encounter there!

His goal is to get more and to live better in comfort... He can even victimize those who are close to him for this purpose. He gives an additional kick to his closest ones while they are still struggling in the swamp of the world, he closes his eyes to the fact that **they keep engaging their brains only with the worldly matters** without doing anything for their life beyond death!..

We do not take it into account that every person comes across with the mischief of Dajjal (Anti-Christ) during his lifetime! We keep waiting for the right-eye-blind-Dajjal to come by the time of Doomsday!..

We do not even realize that **Dajjal's world** is a **person's world that keeps him back from "Allah" and "***khaliphate***"**; and that it is to chose the Dajjal's paradise to employ your brain for the pleasures of this world. We even do not notice that getting prepared for the life beyond death, living "***fiiSabiilAllah***" and attaining the mystery of "***khaliphate***" is one's daring to jump into the **Dajjal's hell fire**!

Because, by showing interest in these subjects for a few hours a week, taking them as a hobby or handling them as a means to ease our conscience, we will only be deceiving ourselves in an excellent way!

* * *

Iman forms one's point of view about life and enables him to perceive all affairs and circumstances with reference to that viewpoint... It generates actions connected with that way of consideration. And you experience the simultaneous effects of your actions depending of what you achieve!..

So is also the lack of faith! You have considerations connected with that point of view, and have actions connected with those considerations and you finally live the effects of them!..

Let us remember again the following advice of the RasulAllah *aleyhessalaam*...

"Allah has created a people for paradise...

Allah has created a people for the hell fire...

The ink of the pen that wrote it, became dry... Every person will find it easy to achieve what has been made easy for him!"

Therefore, my friends, let us realize those facts:

All objects of iman except the *iman* in **"Allah" informed** by RasulAllah, are objects of *iman* requiring to perform actions, based on one's acceptance of life beyond death... While applying those actions, people say "*aslaamnaa*", meaning "**we perform muslim actions**"... But, **they are not believers yet, with reference to the sign in the Koran**!

Those who have faith in Allah through the mystery of "*B*" and who can carry out the required actions "*fiiSabilAllah*" as a natural consequence and who views life with that point of view, are the men of faith (*mumin*) who say "we believe". They have some classes among themselves with reference to their level of insight (*basirat*)... The lowest class is known as "*mutmainna*" (tranquility)!.

Everybody walks towards their purpose of creation and their perfection (*kamal*) with firm steps... However, there are some among us who are set to assuming perfection —full growth (*kamal*)— as to grow roses by planting thistles, and also some who plant rose seed and expect roses!..

Additionally there are the dull-witted (ones with a limited understanding) who are even failing to take into consideration the warnings that have been made to them, while they keep on scattering the thistle seeds thinking that they are planting rose seeds!

In the system and order of Allah, there is no place for excuses. Every person will automatically encounter the consequences of his actions resulting from his viewpoint and his understanding!

If those of tomorrow are making us brood today, they will be putting us in fire tomorrow!

Those who give no heed to the intercession (*shafaat*) today no matter what their excuses are, do not have the right to expect any reward from it!

* * *

LAST WORD

LAST ADVICE

I want to give a **last advice** to some dull-witted and simpleminded acquaintances as well as to those who misunderstand the writings in the **Speeches of the System** including some information in my other publications.

With the grace (*lutf*), benevolence (*ihsan*) and benefaction (*inayat*) of Allah, in addition to the explanations made up to this date by a variety of persons, we have also cited some topics that have not been touched at all.

We have spoken of some points that have not been spoken of before now.

We have referred to some mysteries that have not been revealed before now.

We have suggested some innermost content of the **signs of the Koran**, which have not been highlighted before now.

We have taken up them insofar as foreordained (*taqdir*) for us and made explanations as far as the present circumstances and the science of humanity allowed us to...

However...

Some dull-witted and thick-witted people have drawn misconclusions from all these.

Even they almost went astray to making it lawful (*ibaha*)...

Committing our writings into their memories, they turned to computers full of software packages.

We tried to explain the System; they said they realized the System but they challenged (opposed) the system, and acted on a mentality that fights against it.

We said that one should not stand in front of a roller as it will smash, **they laid themselves before the roller** saying they have realized that "*a roller will smash*"!!!

We said, "**fire burns and water kills by submerging as they never carry a feeling of pity** "...

They jumped into fire or into water saying, "yes we have understood and realized that fire will burn and water will drown", supposing that they had understood (!?) the system!

Woe to them!

What a misunderstanding!

What an unawareness!

What a confusion, misinterpretation!

How can those supposedly men of fashion that are certain of living with reasoning, be so much **irrational**?

I think this is kind of an anti-miracle!

In all my publications, I tried to explain the "DEEN" = the System once again as the Rasul of Allah READ=*IQRAA* and communicated...

I implied the inner dimension of "*salaat*", however I announced it so many times that the inner (*batini*) experiences could only be assessed together with and through the activities of physical brain.

Besides, I tried to tell that "*salaat*" carried out only at the physical (bodily) level will never be complete, and it is necessary to experience its **spiritual (heartful)** = **conscious** effects, as well. Misinterpreting this, some people put the practical effect (physical implementation) of "**five times *salaat***" on a shelf for a rest!

Human being is complete with his **physical body**, **spirit** and **consciousness** (practical, spiritual and conscious aspects) in this world.

All practices known as *ibadat* can reach to perfection with their practical (physical)-spiritual and conscious dimensions of effect altogether.

It is insufficiency to carry out practices known as *ibadat* with only one of its effects. Because, man will ultimately have to pay for his negligence at corresponding dimensions heavily.

This is the effect of the System!

As an **EFFECT OF THE SYSTEM** that **Allah** created, one that does not fulfill what the **Rasul of Allah** stated to fulfill will automatically suffer for a penalty as a return of his missing of that practice.

In the environment that is accessed, man will experience the absence of what he has not taken with himself and will suffer for its painful consequences therein!

No one will judge someone from outside, but everyone will suffer the consequences of what he has not brought about.

<u>In the system and in its operation there is no place for emotionality!</u>

The same way as your physical body automatically suffers the consequences of not taking the necessary medicines when you need them, without its being a punishment by anyone else from outside... And as you can never get the effect of what you failed to carry out, no matter what may be your excuse... **<u>You will automatically live the consequences of failing to assign the required importance and assessment to the PHYSICAL PRACTICES if you disregard them, as they are the necessities of afterlife</u>**... Though it is not a sky-god that will put you in punishment therein, but because of your extreme **impotency,** you will be burned out under the circumstances of the environment you will go into.

Neither **Ahmed Hulusi** nor someone else will be able to deliver you from this!

Because you have chosen the **way of life in this world which means your rejection of the knowledge that** comes to you from the **Rasul of Allah** and reaches **as INTERCESSION** (*shafaat*)!

We have told and written it so many times that "*salaat*", "**fasting**", "*hajj*" and all other proposals are entirely for the advancement of yourself without being for the purpose of pleasing the heart of a god up in the sky!

This is a weak spot of the matter!

Given the information about **the universal SYSTEM within which you will live today and tomorrow**, you are asked to save yourself from the dangers of future with respect to it!

Yet, you say that you understand the system but after all you exhibit **foolishness** by saying, "it would not effect you!"

"**Dougter Fatima, not even I, your father, can deliver you!**" says the **Rasul of Allah**, under the enlightenment of the reality that **SYSTEM IS permanent *sunnat* (fashion) of Allah**... The dull-witted people think that being against (challenging) the system is a level of "**awareness**" (*marifat*)!

Oh you, whose sun is set, stars came down with lights off, who has been sightless, but is still in comfort with the one in his illusion; consoling himself with a self-deception saying "*I can see the mysteries of the universe*"!

Won't you still comprehend the system?

Won't you still perceive that there cannot be a DEEN = SYSTEM that applies to each person differently?

Oh those of you whom I can reach out...

Just for the good of yourself, stick out your heads from your world of illusions inside your cocoon, and realize the **REALITIES OF THE SYSTEM you live within**!

The same way as you become miserable in this world when you conflict with the System, know that you will become miserable **under the effect of the same UNIVERSAL SYSTEM** also **in the realm of afterlife to come**!

Because of your prevailing rejection here, nobody will be able to give you help there!

Whoever opposes the System, will suffer its result heavily!

So should it be known!

* * *

A LAST CHANCE

There is a last chance...

That all that I have written and told up to this date may have been illusions!..

That I have invented all those!

That I was building castles in the air!

That I may have created, written down and communicated what I have made up in my mind only!

God must be sitting in a star in sky and watching people from above...

He must not be in the know of what is inside you!

He must be sort of a character that can be easily fooled and taken in!.

He must be bought off by some bribe when needed!

He must be candid enough to be fooled even by the simpleton, who though cannot even fool the other person!

That God must be done out of sweets and bonbons!

A check or a few pretty girls must be sent to Him to get Him into line if need be!

If you are a Turk who read this writing, He must be the God of Turks; if you are an Arab, he must be a God of Arabs; if a Persian, a God of Persians!.

Your understanding of Religion must be the religion at the sight of that god!

One must be able to lure him and dish up heaven!

People should not be prompted over their funerary box after death saying "*for the chastity of the deceased person...*"! Labels, nobility, official dresses must be of use there and people should be mailed to him with their position, wealth, authority and worldly clothes!

It is a hope!..

It is the hope of those who live on their shrewdness!.

It is the hope of those from a herd who lack the ability to "**READ**", who do not know "**reading**", who is happy with chitchats...

May be it is the case!

But what if it is not?

Oh you, whom the publications of Ahmed Hulusi have reached!..

If all that was written and informed by Ahmed Hulusi are real facts... And if they are only the Truth..?

What if all that Ahmed Hulusi "read" and communicated are true, his explanations being facts and exactly effectual, what will happen in that case?

What if a day is really to come when "**Your wealth and children will make no use**"?

What if a day to come to live in a period after death when "**parents will escape from their children, man and wife from each other and will give damn on themselves**"?

What if there is not a god watching you from above that you may make excuses?

What if you will be losing all the possibility of making something for yourself in the dimension accessed after death, as written by **Ahmed Hulusi**?

What if it is Allah that created you through bringing every atom of you into existence out of Hu's Names?

What if all your actions are accounted for and what if you are living the consequences of your actions in every next moment? And if this is the reason of your unawareness and veiled state!

What if all those staff of life (blessings) that come to you are just DECEPTIONS (**MEKR**) while you enjoy your carnal desires without ever having enough satisfaction?

What if **Ahmed Hulusi** is not ungrateful, mischief-maker, revengeful, immoral, dishonest at all and if the **SYSTEM he communicated is accurate and true**?

What if everyone will receive only the reward of his appreciation of what he learned in this world?

What if the recital of the following statement in the DUA that the **Rasul of Allah** advised us to implement after each time when hearing the "*__adhan__*" (prayer call), is so important:

"Oh Allah whose invitation is COMPLETE and who is the Lord of *salaat* to be implemented..."

What is the COMPLETE invitation?

What does it mean to implement (*iqama*) the *salaat*?

What does it mean to be the LORD of these both? (*See the book DUA and ZHIKR for this dua!*)

What are we required with it?

Why will **Abraham** (peace be upon) him be the **tallest** and the leader of all *muezzin* during the Judgement Day?

If **Angels** will manifest to a man from his internal dimensions rather than the external and if there will not be a god sitting on a throne in front of us nor up in the heavens that could be made excuses, what will befall on us in that case?

What if "**Lordship**" (*Rububiyyat*) is the Lord (*Rabb*) of the realm of actions...

What if actions are manifest only as compositions of Names (*esma*), that is through their "**Lord**"...

Why is it so important to comprehend and experience the composition of Names in you as your *Haqiqat* (Truth), that is your "LORD"?

From whom and into where will you refuge tomorrow if your Lord as the composition of Names in you, works out (settles your accounts) without your notice, as Hu is al **Hasib** (One that counts)?

It is difficult my friend, really difficult!

Even **having faith** (*iman*) is connected with **reasoning** (*aql*)! What if your mind comes short of it?

I never wish to watch you say "*We have passed away the world through deceiving ourselves with false rumors and gossips... Now there is no chance other than suffering its consequences*"!

I never wish to see you say "*I have been taken in by money, my wealth and riches, my family and children, the temporal world tastes and so I have not paid attention to them!*"

I never wish to be an associate today with those who will regret and be wretched tomorrow...

My heart is not suitable for seeing their tomorrows from this day!.

As I have said, there is a **chance**!..

I wish I have been wrong!.

I wish that all that I have written and told in full of books and tapes were to be the works of a daydream!

And people who ignore my explanations were to feel no regret in the life after death!

I am tired, my friend!…

I am exhausted, my friend!..

I am sorry, my friend!..

For you...

For all that I love...

For all that love or not...

For all those that pay no heed to the facts written and communicated for centuries throughout history!..

* * *

Translated by
Ahmed Baki
1999, Istanbul

MOHAMMED'S "ALLAH"

**Allah as Introduced
by
Mohammed**

AHMED HULUSI

The only book on earth that was written to
inform the true understanding of ALLAH as
informed by Mohammed *a.s.*

**Translated by
AHMED BAKI**

www.ahmedbaki.com

Published by KITSAN, Istanbul, TURKEY
Ticarethane Sokak No:41
34400 Cagaloglu - Istanbul / TURKEY
Phone: ++90 212 5136769
Fax: ++90 212 5115144
http://www.kitsan.com

UP TO DATE UNDERSTANDING OF ISLAM

AHMED HULUSI

Shedding light on many misinformation we had, this book essentially aims at making clear the most significant difference in meaning beetween any concept of a "God" and the name "ALLAH", as well as the greatest variance between "Muslimism" and the "RELIGION OF ISLAM".

Translated by
AHMED BAKI

www.ahmedbaki.com

Published by KITSAN, Istanbul, TURKEY
Ticarethane Sokak No:41
34400 Cagaloglu - Istanbul / TURKEY
Phone: ++90 212 5136769
Fax: ++90 212 5115144
http://www.kitsan.com

VIDEO TAPES BY
AHMED HULUSI

(Available in Turkish)

1. **A FRIENDLY CONVERSATION**

2. **GOD OR ALLAH**

3. **LET US KNOW "ALLAH" - 1**

4. **LET US KNOW "ALLAH" - 2**

5. **EXPLANATIONS**

6. **THE TRUTH**

7. **WAKING**

8. **FROM FRIEND TO FRIEND**

9. **SPIRIT - JINN - ANGEL**

10. **QUESTIONS AND ANSWERS**

11. **THE WILL AND DESTINY**

12. **DESTINY AND ASTROLOGY**

13. **A CONFERANCE IN IZMIR**

14. **A CONFERANCE IN ANTALYA**

15. **A CONFERANCE IN FALEZ**

16. **A CONFERANCE IN BEBEK**

AUDIO TAPES BY AHMED HULUSI

(Each 90 minutes conversations, available in Turkish)

1. THE TRUTH OF MAN
2. MAN AND THE AFTER DEATH - 1
3. MAN AND THE AFTER DEATH - 2
4. READING
5. IN ORDER TO BE SAVED
6. AMANTU - 1
7. AMANTU - 2
8. ISLAM
9. THOUGHT OF TRUTH
10. REASONING AND BELIEF
11. ENTRANCE TO ONENESS
12. FUNDAMENTALS OF ONENESS
13. MIRAAJ - ASCENDENCE
14. SPIRITS - MEN - JINN - ANGELS
15. THE HOLY NIGHT OF KADR
16. THE CALIPH OF ALLAH
17. WHAT IS SOUL (NAFS)
18. THE PURIFICATION OF CONSCIOUSNESS
19. AS THE ESSENCE VIEWS
20. THE ORDAINMENT OF THE ONE
21. MATTER OF UPPER DEGREES
22. THE WILL AND THE DESTINY - 1
23. THE WILL AND THE DESTINY - 2
24. DESTINY AND ASTROLOGY

PUBLISHED BOOKS BY AHMED HULUSI

(Available in Turkish unless otherwise specified)

1. **A GUIDE TO SPIRITUAL PRAYINGS**
   First published in 1965
2. **HAZRAT ABU BAKR**
   Printed 6 times since 1967
3. **REVELATIONS**
   Printed 9 times since 1967
4. **SPIRITS - MEN - JINN**
   Printed 15 times since 1972
5. **MYSTERIES OF HUMAN 1-2**
   Printed 17 times since 1986
6. **From FRIEND To Friend**
   (also available in English, German and French translations)
   Printed 8 times since 1987
7. **MOHAMMED'S "ALLAH"**
   (also available in English, German, French, Spanish and Russian translations)
   Printed 16 times since 1989
8. **UNIVERSAL MYSTERIES**
   (English translation available)
   Printed 10 times since 1990
9. **THE INTERPRETATION OF "GHAUSIYYA" BY A.QADIR GEYLANI**
   Printed 7 times since 1991
10. **DUA AND ZHIKR**
    Printed 23 times since 1991
11. **WHAT DID MOHAMMED READ**
    Printed 8 times since 1992
12. **REASONING AND BELIEF**
    Printed 8 times since 1993
13. **MOHAMMED MUSTAFA 1-2**
    Printed 5 times since 1994
14. **KNOW YOURSELF**
    Printed 7 times since 1994

PUBLISHED BOOKS BY AHMED HULUSI

BOOKS ON TAPE BY AHMED HULUSI

(Available in Turkish)

FROM **FRIEND**
TO FRIEND

AHMED HULUSI

Friends Handbook of Sufi
Words of Wisdom

*Open your heart and be inspired by
the Voice of the Universal Essence
that is within all of us.*

Translated by
AHMED BAKI

www.ahmedbaki.com

Published by KITSAN, Istanbul, TURKEY
Ticarethane Sokak No:41
34400 Cagaloglu - Istanbul / TURKEY
Phone: ++90 212 5136769
Fax: ++90 212 5115144
http://www.kitsan.com

THE VOICE OF SYSTEM

AHMED HULUSI

"The Speeches of the Universal System."
A collection of Ahmed HULUSI's most recent
writings from his Internet column...

**Translated by
AHMED BAKI**

www.ahmedbaki.com

Published by KITSAN, Istanbul, TURKEY
Ticarethane Sokak No:41
34400 Cagaloglu - Istanbul / TURKEY
P one: ++90 212 5136769
Fax: ++90 212 5115144
http://www.kitsan.com

UNIVERSAL MYSTERIES

AHMED HULUSI

Open your mind to new horizons and get ready to set out for the discovery of real UNIVERSAL MYSTERIES.

*The ultimate source of wisdom and inspiration descends from the depth of spiritual universe to our physical realm in the appearance of a young man and with the name **Elf**, and answers all the questions in the mind of an intelligent phylosophy teacher **Jamm** during his inner journey to knowing the purpose of life and the Cosmic Consciousness...*

Translated by
AHMED BAKI

www.ahmedbaki.com

Published by KITSAN, Istanbul, TURKEY
Ticarethane Sokak No:41
34400 Cagaloglu - Istanbul / TURKEY
Phone: ++90 212 5136769
Fax: ++90 212 5115144
http://www.kitsan.com

TRUTH OF LIFE

AHMED HULUSI

*What do we know about the world that is
beyond our physical perception?
What does a man's lifetime in this world
amount to if compared to the universal
dimensions of time?
If there is not a god up in the sky who expects
worship from people, then what is the reason of
religious proposals and spiritual practices?
What are we going to experience by death
and beyond death?
What do the Koran and Modern Sciences
say about these subjects?*

Read in this booklet the answers to
these and many more questions, which is
the translation of a script put in writing
from one of Sufi Author Ahmed Hulusi's
audiotapes in Turkish.

Translated by
ALI CUNEYT TARI

Published by KITSAN, Istanbul, TURKEY
Ticarethane Sokak No:41
34400 Cagaloglu - Istanbul / TURKEY
Phone: ++90 212 5136769
Fax: ++90 212 5115144
http://www.kitsan.com